YORK NOTES

A DOLL'S HOUSE

HENRIK IBSEN

Notes by Frances Gray

PEARSON

YORK PRESS

YORK PRESS
322 Old Brompton Road, London SW5 9JH

PEARSON EDUCATION LIMITED
Edinburgh Gate, Harlow,
Essex CM20 2JE, United Kingdom
Associated companies, branches and representatives throughout the world

First published 2008
This new and fully revised edition 2016

10 9 8 7 6

ISBN 978–1–2921–3815–2

Illustration on page 40 by Alan Batley
Phototypeset by Border Consultants
Printed in China (GCC/06)

CONTENTS

PART ONE: INTRODUCING *A DOLL'S HOUSE*

PART TWO: STUDYING *A DOLL'S HOUSE*

PART THREE: CHARACTERS AND THEMES

PART FOUR: GENRE, STRUCTURE AND LANGUAGE

PART FIVE: CONTEXTS AND INTERPRETATIONS

PART SIX: PROGRESS BOOSTER

PART SEVEN: FURTHER STUDY AND ANSWERS

HOW TO STUDY AND REVISE *A DOLL'S HOUSE*

These Notes can be used in a range of ways to help you read, study and revise for your exam or assessment.

Become an informed and independent reader

Throughout the Notes, you will find the following key features to aid your study:

- **Key context** margin features: these widen your knowledge of the setting, whether historical, social or political. This is highlighted by the AO3 (Assessment Objective 3) symbol to remind you of its connection to aspects you may want to refer to in your exam responses.

- **Key interpretation** boxes (a key part of AO5): do you agree with the perspective or idea that is explained here? Does it help you form your own view on events or characters? Developing your own interpretations is a key element of higher-level achievement at A Level, so make use of this and similar features.

- **Key connection** features (linked to AO4): whether or not you refer to such connections in your exam writing, having a wider understanding of how the play, or aspects of it, links to other texts or ideas can give you new perspectives on the text.

- **Study focus** panels: these help to secure your own understanding of key elements of the text. Being able to write in depth on a particular point or explain a specific feature will help your writing sound professional and informed.

- **Key quotation** features: these identify the effect of specific language choices – you could use these for revision purposes at a later date.

- **Progress booster** features: these offer specific advice about how to tackle a particular aspect of your study, or an idea you might want to consider discussing in your exam responses.

- **Extract analysis** sections: these are vital for you to use either during your reading or when you come back to the text afterwards. These sections take a core extract from a chapter and explore it in real depth, explaining its significance and impact, raising questions and offering interpretations.

Stay on track with your study and revision

Your first port of call will always be your teacher, and you should already have a good sense of how well you are doing, but the Notes offer you several ways of measuring your progress.

- **Revision task**: throughout the Notes, there are some challenging, but achievable, written tasks for you to do relevant to the section just covered. Suggested answers are supplied in **Part Seven**.

- **Progress check**: this feature comes at the end of **Parts Two** to **Five**, and contains a range of short and longer tasks which address key aspects of the Part of the Notes you have just read. Below this is a grid of key skills which you can complete to track your progress, and rate your understanding.

- **Practice task** and **Mark scheme**: use these features to make a judgement on how well you know the text and how well you can apply the skills you have learned.

Most importantly, enjoy using these Notes and see your knowledge and skills improve.

The edition used in these Notes is the Bloomsbury Methuen Drama edition, translated by Michael Meyer, 2008.

 **PROGRESS BOOSTER**

You can choose to use the Notes as you wish, but as you read the play it can be useful to read over the **Part Two** summaries and analysis in order to embed key events, ideas and developments in the drama.

AO2 PROGRESS BOOSTER

Don't forget to make full use of **Parts Three** to **Five** of the Notes during your reading of the play. You may have essays to complete on genre, or key themes, or on the impact of specific settings, and can therefore make use of these in-depth sections. Or you may simply want to check out a particular idea or area as you're reading or studying the play in class.

AO1 PROGRESS BOOSTER

Part Six: Progress booster will introduce you to different styles of question and how to tackle them; help you to improve your expression so that it has a suitably academic and professional tone; assist you with planning and use of evidence to support ideas; and, most importantly, show you three sample exam responses at different levels with helpful AO-related annotations and follow-up comments. Dedicating time to working through this Part will be something you won't regret.

A DOLL'S HOUSE: A SNAPSHOT

The shock of the new

A Doll's House ends with a woman slamming a door. It shocked its first audience in 1879 – not just because the woman was walking out on her marriage, but because of the sort of woman she was. Nora Helmer, a middle-class housewife, was exactly the sort of character dramatists did not put on stage. Instead of enjoying an escapist fantasy, the audience found themselves looking into a home like their own – and being encouraged to side with a woman who throws away everything she has been taught about being a wife and mother and declares that she is 'first and foremost a human being' (Act Three, p. 100).

Although it is not easy for us as modern readers to imagine the impact, startling as a cold shower, of this sudden confrontation with modernity, *A Doll's House* continues to challenge and surprise. Where the rights of women are still disputed – indeed in any society where one group has power over another – it has a very direct political energy. But it is also an absorbing story about two people who love each other and find that love is not enough. Both are damaged by the lack of equality in their relationship and Nora must struggle towards a new life.

A star role

The complexity of her struggle makes the role of Nora one of the most rewarding ever written for an actor. There have been many notable Noras, all understanding her differently and asking different questions of the character. For instance, is she tired of playing her husband's 'little squirrel' (Act One, p. 25) from the beginning, or is her childlike behaviour unselfconscious? Does she share the sexual passion her husband Helmer feels for her even though their relationship is unravelling? Twenty-first century Noras may present different answers from those of the pioneering actresses who played her in the nineteenth, but each one has to make decisions about inflections, facial expressions and movements to bring her own Nora alive.

Naturalism: a new style

Ibsen told his wife, Suzannah, that while writing the play he had 'seen' Nora, wearing a 'blue woollen dress' (recounted in Meyer, *Ibsen*, 1985, p. 467). The vividness and clarity with which he imagined ordinary Norwegians like Nora made him the ideal exponent of the emerging theatrical style known as **naturalism**.

Towards the end of the nineteenth century there was a widespread dissatisfaction with existing theatre conventions. Acting had become mannered and false, and situations were contrived for maximum intensity and spectacle. Such a style seemed inappropriate for a scientific age which had invented photography and phonography in order to record the world accurately (see **Historical context**). The French novelist and playwright Émile Zola (1840–1902) coined the term 'naturalism' to define what he wanted on the stage: a way of speaking the truth, in a language that did not demand a special tone of voice and without events that strained credulity.

KEY CONTEXT **A03**

The first print run of the play was sold out even before the play opened in Copenhagen in 1879. Arguments about Nora raged all over Scandinavia. A weary hostess in Sweden wrote on her lunch invitations: 'You are politely requested not to discuss Ibsen's new play' (quoted in *Henrik Ibsen: The Critical Heritage*, edited by Michael Egan, 1972, p. 1).

KEY CONTEXT **A03**

French novelist Émile Zola considered that the battle for naturalism in the novel had been won, but that the stage lagged behind: 'The novel is [naturalism's] domain, its field of battle and of victory ... it is now taking over the stage and is beginning to transform the theatre which is the last stronghold of convention' ('Naturalism in the Theatre', in *Documents of Modern Literary Realism*, edited by George J. Becker, 2015, p. 203).

Close observation and suspense

Naturalism was not about accuracy for its own sake. It wanted to explore the relationship of people's behaviour to their environment. Ibsen was a true original, crafting an absorbing story out of the apparent trivialities of real life – a bag of macaroons, a pair of silk stockings. Instead of listening to characters emoting about their feelings, the audience become detectives. They deduce Nora's state of mind from how she dances, or decorates the Christmas tree. Modern audiences are used to decoding characters like this; the techniques Ibsen developed are still in use, in soap operas and films as well as on stage – but at the first performance in Copenhagen in 1879, the audience would have been working hard to follow the story.

The play could be described as 'the adventures of two hundred and fifty pounds.' This was a substantial sum in the 1870s. **Suspense** rises steadily through the play over a paper which Nora has forged to get money: the Helmers may become social outcasts; their relationship will be radically changed. Their circle encompasses people who have known abject poverty and people to whom money means little, but all of them will be affected by the fate of that paper.

Stereotypes and the rights of women

At the time Ibsen was writing, no woman could vote and it was almost impossible for a woman to get a divorce and keep her children. Many early interpreters of Nora were political activists – including Karl Marx's daughter Eleanor, who played her in 1886 in a private production. It was some years before the strict British censorship of the time allowed public performance in Britain and, as in other countries, a 'happy ending' was imposed, in which Nora stays. Even this, however, could not hide the power of the final scene where husband and wife really talk to each other for the first time. Throughout their marriage they have both performed stereotypical gender roles – sometimes to great comic effect: silly, helpless female and strong, reliable man. Now Nora wants to abandon the mask. Can her husband do the same?

A02

Study focus: Key issues to explore

As you study the text and revise for the exam, keep in mind these key elements:

- How suspense is structured – the shape of the play
- Power relationships – between man and woman, worker and boss
- How characters act (or overact) their gender roles
- The meaning carried by outwardly trivial words or actions
- How text and performer interact to interpret a character
- The function of comedy in a serious play
- How realistic scenery, props and lighting are used to create a world
- Nora's growing understanding of the world and her place in it

A03   **KEY CONTEXT**

One model for Nora was the young novelist Laura Kieler (1849–1932). Like Torvald Helmer, Kieler's husband had been seriously ill, leading her to contract secret debts for a southern holiday. Laura Kieler forged a bank draft; the strain drove her to a breakdown and she was sent to an asylum from which she was discharged into her husband's care. Eleven days later, Ibsen began his notes towards the 'Tragedy of Modern Times' that became *A Doll's House*. Kieler, conservative in her outlook, came to resent her reputation as 'the real Nora'. Joan Templeton gives a detailed account of this episode in *Ibsen's Women* (2001) pp. 135–7.

A05   **KEY INTERPRETATION**

The Irish playwright George Bernard Shaw played Krogstad in the production where Eleanor Marx was Nora. He later wrote that the moment when Nora stops indulging in her emotions, sits down and demands a sensible talk with her husband 'conquered Europe and founded a new dramatic art' (*The Quintessence of Ibsenism*, London, Constable 1913 p. 192).

SYNOPSIS

Act One

A model marriage?

It is Christmas Eve. Nora Helmer arrives home with a Christmas tree and presents for the family. She eats some macaroons. Her husband, Torvald, enters, fretting about her extravagance. Nora points out that his new job as manager of the local bank carries a high salary. She asks for money as her own Christmas present. He teases her as a spendthrift, and asks if she has been eating sweets. She denies it.

A woman with secrets

Two visitors arrive. Helmer retreats to his study to greet their friend Dr Rank; the other caller is Mrs Linde, an old friend of Nora's who wants her to persuade Helmer to employ her at the bank. Mrs Linde compares her financial struggles after the death of her unloved husband with Nora's easy life. Nora claims she too has struggled. Helmer nearly died from overwork and they spent a year in Italy for his health. He refused to pay for the trip and the doctors would not tell him how ill he was. Nora raised the money herself, pretending it was from her father. She has been secretly working to pay off the loan. Another visitor arrives: Nils Krogstad, a clerk at the bank. This troubles Nora, although Krogstad has come to see Helmer. Dr Rank appears and Nora introduces him to Mrs Linde. They discuss 'moral cripple[s]' (p. 39) like Krogstad. Nora becomes excited that Helmer has power over Krogstad. She offers macaroons, pretending they were a gift from Mrs Linde. Helmer returns. He is happy to offer Mrs Linde a job, and leaves with her and Rank.

A looming crisis

Nora plays with her children, but is interrupted by Krogstad. Fearing he will be dismissed by Helmer, he tries to blackmail Nora into using her influence to help him keep his job. It emerges that he was the source of the loan – and Nora forged her father's signature to guarantee it. If she cannot help Krogstad, he will reveal everything. Helmer returns to see Krogstad leaving and assumes that he has come to ask Nora to intercede. Angry when Nora denies this, Helmer announces that liars like Krogstad – and, even worse, 'mothers who are constitutional liars' (p. 53) – damage their children. Alone again, Nora is deeply troubled; she tells their nursemaid that she does not want to see her children.

Act Two

The crisis deepens

It is Christmas Day. The tree is bare. Nora is still troubled. The nurse brings Nora her costume for the fancy dress party that night. Nora asks her how it felt when she left her baby. Mrs Linde arrives and helps to mend the costume, but is bundled out of the room as Helmer arrives – he does not like to watch dressmaking. Nora tries to intercede for Krogstad. Angry, Helmer sends Krogstad a letter of dismissal. Nora pleads with him to change his mind; he patronisingly promises that he is 'man enough' (p. 63) to deal with any trouble.

Lovers or friends?

Dr Rank arrives to tell Nora that he is dying. They flirt over the silk stockings she will wear to the party. Nora tentatively sounds him out for help with the loan. He declares his love. She reproves him and refuses to go on with her request, sending him to visit Helmer. Krogstad arrives, furious at his dismissal, and informs her he now wants a better job. Panicking, Nora contemplates suicide. Leaving, Krogstad puts a note in the locked mailbox, telling Helmer everything.

Dancing for her life

Nora confides in Mrs Linde, who goes to speak to Krogstad, her former lover, on Nora's behalf. Nora babbles about a 'miracle' (p. 74) that must be prevented. She stops Helmer opening the mail, demanding his help rehearsing the tarantella she will dance at the party. As she dances wildly Mrs Linde returns to say Krogstad is out of town. As the curtain falls Nora rushes into Helmer's arms.

Act Three

A different relationship

Mrs Linde is alone at the Helmers' flat. Krogstad arrives. We learn that Mrs Linde had earlier left him for a wealthier man to support her family. He feels his life is a shipwreck, his only comfort the job he has lost – to her. She suggests they 'join hands' (p. 82). She has faith in him and wants to care for him and his children. At first he thinks she wants only a favour for Nora. But when he agrees to ask for his letter back unread, she says that the truth must come out for the sake of Nora's marriage.

Helmer fails Nora

The Helmers return. Helmer is excited at the success of Nora's tarantella and after a drunken lecture to Mrs Linde shows her out, hoping to make love to Nora. Dr Rank arrives – apparently wanting a cigar. He tells Nora in code that the final stage of his disease has begun and leaves. Nora explains his meaning to Helmer, who continues his attentions. She tells him to read his mail. Enraged on reading Krogstad's letter, Helmer declares their marriage is over – although they will stay together for respectability's sake.

A new life

The maid arrives with another letter – from Krogstad, returning the paper with the forged signature. Helmer rejoices that he is saved. Nora goes to remove her fancy dress, while Helmer lectures about forgiveness. She emerges in day clothes, demanding a serious conversation. She accuses Helmer of denying her the chance to grow up, and says she is leaving to educate herself: a 'duty' higher than that of wife or mother (p. 100). When Helmer realises he has lost her love, she explains the 'miracle' she expected – that he would try to take all the blame. When he did not, she felt she had married a 'complete stranger' (p. 102). As Helmer pleads with her, she says that she could only return if their relationship became 'a marriage' (p. 104). Nora leaves. The door slams behind her.

A03 **KEY CONTEXT**

Quite early in his career, Ibsen had the job of creating a Norwegian National Theatre in Bergen. Directing plays, he greatly disliked the sets available to him, which had painted furniture on a backcloth rather than real items. His careful stage directions show his concern that the stage should be full of practical (real) things to be used in the play, rather than simply providing background for the actors to pose against. You will find that many items, such as the piano and the Christmas tree, have significant roles in the action.

A03 **KEY CONTEXT**

Ibsen's concern for convincing and solid objects on stage was shared by his contemporary, the Swedish playwright August Strindberg (1849–1912). In the preface to his play *Miss Julie* (1888) Strindberg complained that the canvas scenery made it impossible for 'an angry father to express his fury ... by slamming the door.' The slam is central to *A Doll's House*, but Ibsen locates it offstage, possibly to ensure that it is always convincing however poorly constructed the set.

ACT ONE PART ONE: PAGES 23–8

Summary

- Nora Helmer arrives home with her Christmas shopping.
- While her husband is in his study, she nibbles some macaroons.
- Helmer enters to discuss household expenses. She is hopeful about his new job.
- He insists they must wait till his salary arrives before they spend any of it.
- He teases her about eating sweets.
- Visitors arrive. Helmer is not pleased.

Analysis

The curtain rises

Ibsen's choice of title suggests the location is important, and he gives us a chance to look at the 'house' without the characters while Nora is making her way upstairs. Stage **naturalism** – the representation of plausible situations on sets designed to look as **realistic** as possible – was a novelty in the 1870s. This is only Ibsen's second play of contemporary life. The audience would be used to more aristocratic locations, and would have been interested in the clues that suggest this is a new kind of play.

The set shows that this is a household with some pretensions to culture – the engravings point to an interest in art. The piano, an expensive item of furniture, suggests modest prosperity. The audience might also have expectations on observing that the room has four doors. Popular drama of the period depended on intrigue. So many entrances to a single living room suggests that, at some point, characters may be hiding. In fact Nora's first word is 'Hide' (p. 23).

Domestic comedy

The Christmas tree, Nora's high spirits and her generosity to the porter all imply that this will be a domestic **comedy** and that its intrigues will be light-hearted. This is reinforced by the first real laugh of the play. Helmer has no intention of leaving his study simply to greet his wife. Then he registers her remark 'see what I've bought' (p. 24). It brings him popping out like a bird from a cuckoo clock. This is a variation on a comic device, the **double take**, where someone briefly ignores important information before shock suddenly dawns. The laughter springs from the actor's rapid change of expression.

Here, his rush to the door marks Helmer as a potential figure of fun, fussy about money. There seems to be no real threat of poverty. The difference shown here in male and female attitudes to spending seems to involve the kind of comic stereotyping we can still see in the more old-fashioned kind of TV sitcom. Helmer's names for his wife – 'skylark' and 'squirrel' (p. 24) – sound patronising. Nora has no nickname for him. However, her line 'if you only knew what expenses we larks and squirrels have' (p. 26) suggests the animal names are a private joke in a happy relationship. Helmer labours the point that Nora is impractical, but he manages a small joke, that she saves every penny she can: 'But you can't' (p. 26). It all seems consistent with a light comedy about a dizzy young wife with a sensible husband. Ibsen's first Nora, Betty Hennings, was famous for exactly this kind of role.

KEY CONTEXT **A03**

Although Scandinavia is a land of pine forests, the Christmas tree is a German custom and had only recently become popular in Ibsen's Norway. They were quite expensive to buy. Nora's tree is an indication of modest wealth – it might well be the first she has ever bought. It indicates her desire to enjoy their new prosperity, in contrast to the relative poverty of the previous year.

KEY CONTEXT **A03**

Nora's idea of wrapping up some banknotes in gold paper (p. 26) is like the running joke between Ibsen and his wife, Suzannah. He would make elaborately decorated 'banknotes' for her from the 'National Bank of Ibsen', which he replaced with real money when he had sold some of his work. Several of these have survived.

Study focus: Warning signs

Look for indications of deeper issues beneath the comic surface. Before we see Nora, the bell to the flat rings. Does Nora not have her own key? She seems reluctant to open or knock on Helmer's door. Although she is confident and shows no signs of awkwardness, there is also a sense that she is not fully mistress of her house. And while Helmer teases her as a 'squanderbird' (p. 26), his feelings about her extravagance appear to be deep-seated. He sees it not simply as the silliness of a giddy young woman but as a weakness inherited from her father: 'It's in your blood' (p. 26). This leads the audience to wonder if Nora may have a more painful past than her present happy manner implies.

The exchange also makes it clear that, although Nora is willing to charm Helmer to get what she wants, she is happy to contradict him. 'I wish I'd inherited more of papa's qualities' (p. 27) is not the sweetly compliant reply Helmer might prefer.

Food for thought

Helmer finds a topic of conversation where he feels he can take the moral high ground. He tells Nora she looks 'awfully guilty' (p. 27) and begins to interrogate her about eating sweets. There is considerable comic potential in this episode. Macaroons are crumbly delicacies with a creamy centre – they are not easy to eat tidily. Nora's struggles to conceal her forbidden treat will be amusing. Helmer's first teasing remarks are also comic – but when he adds 'you've given me your word' (p. 27) there is a hint that all may not be well with the marriage. There seems to be a worrying lack of trust here and his reaction to the arrival of visitors – 'What a bore' (p. 28) – is somewhat out of keeping with the Christmas spirit Nora has established with her tree and talk of presents. Does Helmer want to keep her all to himself?

Key quotation: The role of money

Helmer announces, 'A home that is founded on debts and borrowing can never be a place of freedom and beauty' (p. 25).

This pompous statement sounds like a favourite saying of Helmer's rather than a spontaneous thought. With no welfare system in place, the first audiences would well understand his fear of debt. But given his controlling behaviour in this scene, his description of home as a 'place of freedom' is **ironic**. The line is an early hint that money and debt will play a central part in the action of the play.

Revision task 1: First impressions

Make brief notes about what you have learned about the main characters by this point in the play. Write about:

- Your first impressions of Nora and Helmer
- Who seems at this point to be the more practical character

A05 KEY INTERPRETATION

Carrie Cracknell directed a notable production of *A Doll's House* at the Young Vic in 2012. She and her star, Hattie Morahan, also made a short film for the internet, *Nora*, exploring the pressures on women today. While the modern Nora in the film has a responsible job, she struggles to look after the house, the bills, and three children; when she reaches the office, the boss announces that he is going to his daughter's school concert. A co-worker grovels, 'I honestly don't know how you manage to fit it all in, I really don't.'

A01 PROGRESS BOOSTER

There are a great many objects (**properties**) on stage in this scene and they have a definite effect. For example, Nora displays her choice of Christmas presents for the children and servants. The children's toys are geared to gender stereotypes, while the maids receive useful rather than enjoyable gifts. It is worth listing the props required throughout the play and reflecting on what they might say about the characters.

ACT ONE PART TWO: PAGES 28–39

Summary

- While Helmer goes into the study with Dr Rank, Nora talks to her old friend Mrs Linde.
- Mrs Linde asks Nora to use her influence with Helmer to get her a job.
- Nora tells Mrs Linde her secret – she borrowed money to pay for Helmer's convalescence, and has been working to pay off the debt.
- Krogstad, a clerk at the bank, comes to see Helmer. Nora is disturbed when she sees him.

Analysis

Contrasting characters

Initially, the two female characters seem to contrast sharply. Although they were at school together, Mrs Linde looks older. Her clothes probably show that she is poor, and a widow. Nineteenth-century mourning conventions were strict and she would wear shabby black or grey. Her rather envious remarks suggest she thinks Nora is stylishly dressed. However, we will learn that there is a secret behind the elegant dress. Clothes will have an important role in the play. Mrs Linde's garments also indicate that she has been travelling. Nora, on the other hand, looks like a housewife. She fusses about chairs and – as she often does – drifts to the stove, in search of warmth and comfort.

Mrs Linde's function in this scene is a traditional one – she is a **confidante**. Her dramatic function is to listen to the heroine's secrets. However, Ibsen gives her an unusually active role: she has her own story. She has actually faced poverty and bereavement; we have just heard Helmer jokingly outline a similar fate for Nora if he should die before his new salary arrived and she had debts. That may make us, as well as Nora, inclined to respect the practical Mrs Linde.

Women and work

Mrs Linde values work for its own sake. Nora is soon boasting that she too is 'proud and happy' (p. 34) about earning money. Her sense of rivalry with her old friend is comic, but this section is important. It shows Mrs Linde as a mirror in which Nora could view herself: not as she is, but as the independent woman she is capable of becoming. Although Nora has not faced the struggles of Mrs Linde, both women clearly feel that self-reliance is a good quality for a woman. Nora sounds envious of Mrs Linde's confidence as a traveller, taking a long trip alone by steamer in the depths of winter. They certainly do not think – as social conventions would require – that work is degrading to women. Nora has relished earning money – 'like being a man' (p. 37). We can see that, although Nora has only just begun her journey to independence, both of these characters are modern women.

Progress booster: Shifting impressions

Nora's revelations to Mrs Linde mean that we need to rethink our understanding of her. We have perhaps assumed that Helmer is correct when he reproves her for extravagance. In fact, she must have been managing her finances exceptionally well. Her initial happiness may be prompted by the prospect of paying off the debt more easily than she had expected, rather than by pleasure in spending money on presents.

We may also have assumed that Nora is rather incompetent – Helmer teases her about ruining last year's Christmas decorations through carelessness; now it is clear that she was only pretending to make them while working as a copyist. Even her clothes may look different to us, once we see them as clever bargains rather than expensive luxuries. It is part of Ibsen's technique as a playwright to surprise us constantly, not just with twists in the plot but by changing our view of the characters – or their view of themselves. Look out for other examples of this technique as you read through the play.

Childish adults

The silliness Nora assumes when cajoling Helmer for money is clearly a conscious performance, but can be interpreted in different ways. She may enjoy playing the 'squirrel' as a relief from Helmer's stuffiness. Perhaps their games allow both of them the relief of being childish for a while, and Nora's persona evidently evokes desire in Helmer. We also discover that Helmer is less mature than he first appeared. The doctors had turned to Nora to explain just how ill he was – he evidently lacks the strength of character to deal with information like this. He had made himself ill through overwork, in contrast to his wife, who seems to be thriving on it. Nora also fears that his ego cannot cope with the idea that he has depended on her, even unknowingly, for money.

A vulnerable marriage

While Helmer is the head of the house in the eyes of society, the Law and the Church, it seems that the balance of strength in the marriage is rather different. Nora gives us our first hint that this imbalance makes it less secure than first appeared. In one of her confidences to Mrs Linde, she envisages a time when 'it no longer amuses him to see me dance and dress up and play the fool for him' (p. 36) and she intends to keep Helmer by evoking his gratitude for saving his life. This is not quite consistent with the fear she has just expressed that he could not bear dependency on a woman. It may be that Nora is deceiving herself – or she may realise, on some level, that both of them need to become more adult.

The plot advances

The arrival of Krogstad, and the very different reactions of both women to his fleeting appearance, creates **suspense**. He has no obvious connection with the action so far, but it is clear that this new character is important and we can expect new revelations.

Key quotation: Nora's capacity for change

Nora tells her guests, 'it's a wonderful thing to be alive and happy' (p. 38). The vitality that spills out of Nora is not only attractive, but prepares us for the possibility that this is a story about a woman's transformation.

A04 KEY CONNECTION

In 1894 George Bernard Shaw wrote *Candida* as a companion piece to *A Doll's House*. The heroine must choose between the young poet who idolises her and her husband, James. She chooses 'the weaker of the two' – James, a dynamic social reformer whose ego depends on female support: 'Ask James's mother and his three sisters what it cost to save James the trouble of doing anything but be strong and clever and happy. Ask me what it costs to be James's mother and three sisters and mother and wife and mother to his children all in one.' (Shaw, *Plays*, Signet Classics, 1960, p. 233)

A05 KEY INTERPRETATION

Unlike novels and poems, where the reader can re-read earlier material, a play must work as an experience in time. The playwright must not only give the audience information, but decide the best point for them to receive it. You might consider how differently we would interpret this first act if we knew Nora's secret from the beginning.

ACT ONE PART THREE: PAGES 39–43

Summary

- Dr Rank arrives. Nora introduces Dr Rank and Mrs Linde. The doctor is in bad health.
- They discuss Krogstad, who is still with Helmer. He is described by Dr Rank as a 'moral cripple' (p. 39).
- The discussion broadens to include society as a whole. Nora is bored and passes round macaroons.
- Helmer offers Mrs Linde a job at the bank, and leaves with the visitors.
- The nurse returns with the children. Nora plays happily with them.

Analysis

Social responsibility

After the quiet duologues, the stage is suddenly busy. All the arrivals and departures seem at first to have little dramatic purpose beyond prolonging **suspense**. The audience will be curious to know why Nora is uncomfortable at the presence of Krogstad, but will have to wait for the explanation – she clearly will not tell her guests. However, a theme is beginning to emerge: responsibility. Dr Rank and Mrs Linde conduct a short debate, which uses Krogstad as an example. Should a responsible society tolerate his moral lapse and give him a chance to redeem himself through honest work? Or does this merely deprive a better man of a job? We do not, of course, know any details of Krogstad's offence. But the debate reveals something of the way the characters think. Mrs Linde, who knows Krogstad, seems prepared to argue the case for a world that offers second chances; we may wonder what their relationship has been. The doctor, himself 'wretched' and 'tortured' (p. 39) by poor health, perhaps resents the idea that the morally weak should get so much attention.

A moral test

Nora claims to be bored by this rather abstract discussion. However, as she starts to distribute macaroons, her guests are confronted with a dilemma. They know Helmer has forbidden macaroons. Will they take responsibility for telling Helmer? Or will they conceal the truth? Despite the upright tone of their debate, the doctor and the independent working woman gobble the macaroons. They suddenly look as childish as Nora. When Helmer enters, they keep quiet. This tiny comic moment suggests that taking responsibility for one's actions, or owning up to a lie, is not easy.

Key quotation: Nora's world   **A01**

Previously, when Helmer mentioned showing responsibility to the people they might borrow money from, Nora called them 'strangers' (p. 25). Now, when the debate turns to 'society', she remarks, 'What do I care about society? I think it's a bore' (p. 40). However, it is worth bearing in mind that Nora does seem to have close relationships, while Helmer complains about visitors – it is Nora who buys presents; it is Nora who feeds her guests. It can be argued that her words show the narrowness of her experience rather than selfishness.

KEY CONTEXT   **A03**

When Dr Rank describes Krogstad as 'announcing, as though it were a matter of enormous importance, that he had to live' (p. 39), he is quoting Voltaire (François-Marie Arouet, 1694–1778), a writer admired by Ibsen. A supporter of social reform, Voltaire spoke out despite the strict censorship laws and harsh penalties for those who broke them. When a man asked him for money 'because I have to live', he replied: 'I don't see the necessity'. Voltaire's cynicism and concern for justice both fit the character of Dr Rank. The quotation establishes him as an educated but not idealistic man.

KEY CONTEXT   **A03**

The relationship between crime and sickness was hotly debated during the nineteenth century. Those who subscribed to Darwin's theory of evolution, for example, might have seen the criminal as an unhealthy specimen doomed to die out, rather than as a person with sole responsibility for his actions. The debate about Krogstad as a 'moral cripple' shows that Dr Rank keeps up with scientific developments.

Study focus: A complex symbol

A02

Note that, like many stage **props** in the play, the macaroons have a complex function. Bright and colourful, they show Nora's childish side and make us laugh at her greed. They hint that she finds self-control difficult: 'Just a little one. Two at the most' (p. 40). This, of course, underlines the strength she has needed to deprive herself of luxuries while paying off the debt. The macaroons also reveal her willingness to deceive Helmer – even, like Eve with the apple, to tempt others to do so, as she shares them with Mrs Linde and Dr Rank.

In this episode the macaroons seem to give Nora energy; she is amusingly like a child with a sugar rush. But excessive eating can also be a symptom of suppressed rage. She suddenly confesses an urge to swear in front of Helmer – though when challenged to do so by Dr Rank, she cannot get the words out. Rank and Mrs Linde are mildly shocked at her expletive – but interestingly, they do not enquire *why* she wants to say it. It may be that they think she is simply experimenting with shocking language as a child might do. But in Rank's case at least, silence on the subject may mean that he is fully aware that Helmer can be a controlling and difficult man. When Nora eats too many sweets, she may be **symbolically** 'eating her words'. It helps her switch her language into a different register as Helmer enters and she becomes the cajoling child to help Mrs Linde secure her job.

Progress booster: Motherhood

A03

Note how the arrival of the children widens the debate on responsibility to include the question of duty to the family. You will see this becoming a key issue for Nora as the play goes on. While fathers of the period had less engagement with childcare than today, Helmer seems comically anxious to offload them, rushing off with 'Come, Mrs Linde. This is for mothers only' (p. 43). It has to be said that this is not the most sensitive of remarks: Nora has taken the trouble to find out that Mrs Linde has no children and is sorry this is so, but Helmer simply assumes that a woman who works would be childless.

Nora, on the other hand, is keen to be with her children, dancing with them, cuddling them and taking off their wet things. Her concern for the nurse's comfort here shows her to be a considerate employer. Ibsen's lines and detailed stage directions should be taken as a series of cues for the actor to improvise with the children. They allow her to give an impression of ease and childlike spontaneity. It is clear that, although the nurse is important to her, Nora is a devoted and experienced mother. As the play goes on, the audience may become sharply divided in their views about Nora's choices as a parent, but her maternal feelings are clearly genuine.

ACT ONE PART FOUR: PAGES 43–51

Summary

- Nora gets a shock as Krogstad walks in on her games with the children.
- We learn that Krogstad is the man from whom she borrowed the money.
- He tells Nora that Helmer may dismiss him from the bank. He mentions that in the past he did something dishonest.
- He asks Nora to use her influence with Helmer to help him keep his job.
- We learn that Nora forged her father's signature on the paper guaranteeing a loan. Krogstad threatens to go to the police if she does not do what he asks.
- Nora feels unable to be with her children, and begins to decorate the tree.

Analysis

Developing popular drama

In this part of Act One Ibsen uses some themes from the popular drama of his day. Blackmail, compromising documents and villainous moneylenders were the stock-in-trade. Ibsen directed dozens of such plays. Though he despised them, he shows the same adroit manipulation of **suspense** in this section. There have been several tantalising hints that Krogstad will be a major player in the story, and the audience will be excited to learn how. We have assumed that he left with Helmer, so his entrance is a surprise. Ibsen even heightens the tension a little more by first making it clear that Krogstad has not, as Nora imagines, simply come early for the latest instalment of his money, encouraging us to wonder about his **motivation**.

A new aspect of Nora

The tone of this scene is very distinctive in its **naturalism**. There are no heroes or villains. Both characters are complex and fallible. We may instinctively side with Nora as she is so afraid in the first moments. But she promptly reveals a snobbish discourtesy towards Krogstad as a member of an inferior class: 'one of my husband's employees' (p. 45). And she tells the children he is a 'strange gentleman' (p. 44). We have already learned that, for Nora, 'stranger' is a term of dislike. Her rudeness arises from her knowledge that she will no longer have to struggle to pay off the debt: 'Once the New Year is in, I'll soon be rid of you' (p. 46). It has not occurred to her that the man she has made use of may have feelings of his own. He is evidently part of the 'society' she finds 'a bore' (p. 40).

An unlikely stage villain

Blackmailers in popular plays of the period demanded large sums of money, or sex, from the helpless heroine. But all Krogstad wants is respectability – in fact, **ironically** enough, he wants to be just like Helmer. He wants to put his slightly shady past behind him and keep the respect of his children. Nora's insults – 'filthy, beastly' (p. 47) – perhaps provoke him to make more powerful threats than he intended.

Key quotation: Krogstad's motivation **A01**

Krogstad's warning, 'I shall fight for my little job at the bank as I would fight for my life' (p. 46) is curiously touching. Work is as important to Krogstad as it is to Mrs Linde, or indeed to Nora.

Ibsen's exposition

It is worth noting the skill with which Ibsen organises the **exposition** here. It is important that the audience understands exactly the kind of trouble Nora is in, and Krogstad takes Nora through the events of the recent past step by step. However, the complex emotions of the characters ensure that we never feel irritated by the fact that he is telling her things that logically she must know already.

Krogstad seems to be going into this level of detail in order to torment Nora for her rudeness. Instead of challenging her at once, he allows her to lie and claim that her father signed the paper to guarantee the loan. He even hints that he is sympathetic to the strain she was suffering over her father's illness: 'That was a very difficult time for you just then' (p. 48). Only then does he come to the point: 'Your father died on the twenty-ninth of September. But look at this. Here your father has dated his signature the second of October' (p. 48). Nora's persistent silence until Krogstad points out that he 'seems to know' the handwriting is almost comic. We have already seen her lying over small things to Helmer and here she seems like a naughty child confronted with some undeniable evidence. Her bold admission that she did forge the signature comes as a surprise.

A change in the conversation

We may well have lost respect for Nora after her earlier display of snobbery. Her courage in speaking the truth restores it. Krogstad, too, now seems to regard her differently. Instead of treating her like a child, as Helmer does, needling her with questions to which he probably knows the answer, he seems genuinely curious as to why she did not get her dying father to sign the paper. When he charges her with dishonesty towards himself she continues to be snobbish and rude. However, he does not sneer at her naïveté in thinking that the law would take into account her desire to spare her father pain and save her husband. Rather, he simply tells her the truth: 'The law does not concern itself with motives.' (p. 49)

Study focus: Another mirror for Nora **A02**

In this scene, note how Krogstad tries to make clear to Nora that she has committed 'no bigger nor worse a crime than the one I once committed' (p. 49). Although his intent here is to stress that he is implacable and that she is in danger, his phrasing is interesting. Rather than rejoicing that she is no better than he is, he seems concerned that she should not judge him. Like Mrs Linde, Krogstad is a mirror in which Nora can view herself. If the independent woman showed her what she could become, Krogstad is the scared and deceitful person she will be if she does not face her problem. It is not surprising that his exit prompts a flurry of activity on Nora's part. She decorates the Christmas tree not only to distract herself from anxiety, but to resume the role of pretty and carefree wife she knows how to play.

A03 **KEY CONTEXT**

One of Ibsen's earliest notes on *A Doll's House*, dated October 19th 1878, says, 'There are two kinds of spiritual laws ... one for men and one for women.' Nora seems to think that her first duty had been to her loved ones and evidently feels no guilt over forging her father's signature. Is Ibsen suggesting that men and women have different moral instincts? Or does Nora feel as she does because she lacks the education to know the law?

A05 **KEY INTERPRETATION**

In the Methuen Student edition of the play, Nick and Non Worrall note that Nora has dated the document after her father was dead. They suggest that she has not attempted to copy his handwriting, but signed his name on his behalf with no intent to deceive. Ibsen is ambiguous here and the choice the actor makes will affect the whole performance. If she assumes that Nora made some effort to imitate her father's writing, she will underline Nora's resemblance to Krogstad the forger; if she assumes Nora has not done this, she will be playing the character as more naive and foolish.

ACT ONE PART FIVE: PAGES 51–4

Summary

- As Nora decorates the tree, Helmer returns and asks if anyone has called at the house. Nora lies.
- Helmer has seen Krogstad and lectures Nora about lying.
- She diverts him with talk about the coming party.
- Helmer explains that, as a liar, Krogstad will corrupt his own children.
- Troubled, Nora refuses to see her own children.

Analysis

A creature in a cage

Just like Krogstad's forceful arrival to blackmail Nora, Helmer's entry is a surprise. Rather than the cheerful room where Nora has welcomed visitors, the space is beginning to resemble a trap in which she is helpless. Helmer's questions reinforce this impression. He is clearly trying to catch Nora out. As he continues to pressure her, she even admits to things that are not true – Krogstad did *not* ask her to conceal his visit. Helmer seems more anxious to put Nora in the wrong than to think about Krogstad. It does not seem to trouble him that pretending not to know if anyone had been to the house is both mean-spirited and dishonest. His use of the 'songbird' image (p. 51) stresses Nora's status as a pet – and a creature in a cage. A submissive and therefore truthful wife is an important part of the furniture of his peaceful home.

Progress booster: Silences **A01**

Look out for silences that say as much as speech. Nora's pause (p. 53) as she decorates the tree in front of Helmer is important. We have already learned from her short **soliloquy** before his entrance that it is part of her plan to do everything to please Helmer (p. 51). In this silence we realise the tree no longer gives her pleasure, as it did at the start of the play – rather she is using a break in the conversation to plan how to introduce the topic of Krogstad.

Manipulating the conversation

Nora begins to weave the subject of Krogstad in and out of a discussion about her projected fancy dress. The contrast between the childlike creature Helmer imagines her to be, and the desperate but resourceful woman she is, is increasingly marked. She begins the conversation about the party to distract Helmer. However, the line 'It all seems so stupid and meaningless' (p. 52) is a strong statement that does not really fit the topic of fancy dress. It suggests that she is offering Helmer a cue to enter a different conversation. Perhaps she intends to mention Krogstad, or even speak about the wider issues raised by Dr Rank and Mrs Linde in their talk about society. Whatever her intent, Helmer crushes it with his patronising reply: 'So my little Nora has come to that conclusion, has she?' (p. 52) As Helmer reveals his strategy to reorganise the bank, we see Nora realise something else – that Krogstad too is under pressure. Her comment 'this poor man' (p. 52) may reflect dawning compassion for the 'stranger', as well as an attempt to influence her husband.

Shifts in mood

Nora's instant switch to the topic of fancy dress at Helmer's 'Hm!' (p. 52) suggests that she is well acquainted with Helmer's temper and how far it can be tried. Clearly the only way to return to the subject of Krogstad is to make it obvious she is incapable of independent thought and allow Helmer to shape the conversation. So she lays on the flattery so thickly that it seems almost certain Helmer will be suspicious. His line 'Aha! Little Miss Independent's in trouble' (p. 52) comes as a wonderfully comic confirmation that she has judged his egotism correctly.

Ibsen then abruptly changes the mood. So far Helmer has been vague about the details of Krogstad's misdemeanour and Nora perhaps expects him to be so again. However, he spells out the nature of Krogstad's crime – and it is exactly the same as Nora's own. Nora's horror is reflected in the breathless short questions that follow. She cannot now comfort herself with the idea that Krogstad has been simply trying to frighten her.

Study focus: The power of naturalism

Note what is happening on stage at this point. The **irony** of Helmer's talk about liars shows Ibsen handling with great assurance one of the developing conventions of **naturalistic** theatre: apparently casual words spoken by one character which have a devastating effect on another. From Helmer's viewpoint, his remark, 'Nearly all young criminals are the children of mothers who are constitutional liars' (p. 53) is just an opportunity to show off his skill in argument. He expects Nora to be impressed. She, however, fresh from the debate between Dr Rank and Mrs Linde, is genuinely afraid that she could corrupt her children. Ibsen's stage direction tells the actress playing Nora to come *'closer behind him'* (p. 53) – hence her husband cannot see the look on her face, but we can.

A powerful curtain

Helmer effectively manipulates Nora into promising that she will drop the subject of Krogstad. By forcing her to shake hands, he is making her give her word to do so. He has previously made her give her word not to eat sweets. It seems that he expects to control her behaviour in serious as well as trivial matters. Nora, however, is physically and mentally agitated, complaining how 'hot' it is (p. 54). When she refuses to allow the nurse to bring the children in to see her, it is clear that she is not just afraid of what Krogstad may do; she is now afraid of herself. As the curtain falls, the audience will not only wonder how the blackmail plot will play out, but how this woman who has already begun to change will deal with the new and frightening idea that her crime may have made her an unfit mother for her children.

A05   KEY INTERPRETATION

The critic and playwright William Archer made excellent translations of Ibsen's plays and was involved in many productions. He also wrote a book called *Play-making: A Manual of Craftsmanship* (1912) – a helpful analysis of how the plays of Ibsen and his contemporaries are constructed. He describes the need for a convincing ending to the first act of a play, which he says is 'the point at which the drama, hitherto latent, plainly declares itself'. At this point we know enough about the Helmers' marriage and Nora's financial situation to realise that her life is likely to change irrevocably, though we do not yet know how.

A05   KEY INTERPRETATION

In 1983 the critic Elizabeth Hardwick wrote a noted essay in the *New York Review of Books* describing the main emotions driving the action of Ibsen's plays as 'resentment and grievance'. Krogstad here is clearly motivated by both of these. We might also ask whether Nora is beginning to resent Helmer for his stubborn refusal to borrow money for his holiday and his even more stubborn attitude towards Krogstad.

KEY CONTEXT **A03**

At age eighteen Ibsen had an affair with a servant girl, Else Jensdatter, who became pregnant. Wretchedly poor at the time, he paid to support their son, Hans Jacob Henriksen, and continued to do so for fourteen years, although he probably never met him. Issues of paternity and illegitimacy occur in several of his plays, such as *The Wild Duck*, though the nurse's story is perhaps the most poignant of all.

KEY CONNECTION **A04**

A. S. Byatt's novel *The Biographer's Tale* (2001) explores Ibsen's preoccupation with doubles and characters who mirror one another – like Nora and her mirrors Krogstad, Mrs Linde and the nurse. Byatt imagines an encounter between Ibsen and his illegitimate son, Hans Jacob, who is sitting in Ibsen's special chair in his favourite café, dressed in one of his father's own discarded suits. Hans Jacob quotes from several of Ibsen's plays dealing with the subject of heredity.

ACT TWO PART ONE: PAGES 55–60

Summary

- It is Christmas Day. The nurse fetches the costume Nora is to wear to the fancy dress party.
- Nora asks the nurse whether she misses the child she gave up in order to come and be Nora's own nurse.
- Mrs Linde arrives, and offers to mend the costume.
- They discuss Dr Rank's illness. Mrs Linde warns Nora about her closeness to him.
- Nora explains that Dr Rank is not the source of the loan.
- Helmer returns, and Mrs Linde is bustled out of the room.

Analysis

The passage of time

Note how Ibsen uses the set to convey some important information. The tree is stripped of its presents, the candles are burnt out. We are left to imagine what the daytime festivities might have been like. We have already seen Nora creating a façade of happiness when decorating the tree – perhaps she has managed to make the day cheerful and hide her feelings. The tree's present state reminds us that time is running out – Nora can assume that Krogstad cannot send the paper to Helmer on a holiday, but it is nearly over. We also notice Nora's cloak on the sofa. Is she planning to run away? She will not use her outdoor clothes in the scene, which certainly adds to the impression that she is caught in a trap. Her words, 'It couldn't happen' (p. 55), reflect those at the end of the first act. It gives the impression that she may have spent twenty-four hours obsessively repeating her fears in her mind.

Study focus: The nurse – another Nora   **A02**

The nurse is yet another figure in the hall of mirrors in which Nora finds herself trapped. Although the nurse's role is small, this is an important scene. It shows a moment of simple love, in contrast to the game-playing and self-deception at the heart of the Helmers' marriage. It also brings into the play the wider world of female experience. The nurse's story is tragic, but her matter-of-fact tone about girls who 'got into trouble' (p. 56) and her touchingly low expectations (two letters in a period as long as Nora's own lifetime) remind us that such stories are common in the 'society' everyone has been glibly discussing.

Although they have been together for a long time, this seems to be the first time Nora has asked the nurse about her past life. She is beginning to take note of 'society' and show interest in other people. She is also aware of her own vulnerability. Helmer's condemnation of lying mothers has evidently led her to think about leaving her children for their own good. Although Nora is materially better off than the nurse, both women are equally powerless under the law. If there were a divorce, Helmer would be given custody.

Dressing up

Nora's outburst about her fancy clothes – 'I wish I could tear them into a million pieces!' (p. 55) – reflects her earlier comment to Helmer that 'It all seems so stupid and meaningless' (Act One, p. 52). This suggests that the dress is acquiring a **symbolic** significance for her. Helmer's choice of a Neapolitan fisher-girl's outfit may reflect his sense of social superiority to Nora. We can infer that, like most bourgeois men of his day, he sees a non-working wife as proof of his status. The clothes of a working woman are 'fancy dress'. The costume is also a souvenir of the Italian holiday for which Nora has gone into debt. Helmer 'had it made' for her, (p. 57) and possibly paid for dancing lessons too. Clearly he spared no expense, innocently adding to the strain on Nora.

Mrs Linde says that she would like to see her 'dress up' in it (p. 57). In the original Norwegian the same word is used to describe decorating the Christmas tree. Nora is perhaps growing weary of 'dressing up' for Helmer as his social and sexual inferior, and of being 'dressed up' like a doll by him. The appearance of the tree she bought earlier, now stripped of its finery and unwanted, is a reminder of the fears Nora expressed to Mrs Linde earlier about being 'no longer pretty' (Act One, p. 36).

The limits of female knowledge

Practical and optimistic, Mrs Linde turns her hand to repairing the dress. Given what she knows about Nora's debts, it may be that she thinks she is also helping to mend potential problems in Nora's marriage. However, she makes some assumptions that suggest she does not altogether understand her friend. It shocks her a little to find that Nora knows so much about Dr Rank's hereditary illness. Once she has established that her friend has worldly knowledge about sexuality and disease, she goes on to take for granted that Nora's loan has come from Dr Rank, and hints his motive for it must be a sexual one. Mrs Linde is thinking in theatrical clichés; the situation is more interesting than this. Like many girls in the nineteenth century, Nora may have been deprived of education to preserve her 'innocence' – but she does value and apply the knowledge that she has. Dr Rank treats her like an adult because he likes her.

Key quotation: Male sensibility **A01**

Nora worries that 'Torvald can't bear to see sewing around' (p. 60) – so Mrs Linde is hurried offstage as if she were a character in a **farce**. While the episode is comic, it also shows the tendency of everyone except Krogstad to pander to Helmer's whims.

A05 **KEY INTERPRETATION**

One of the engravings prominent on the wall of the Helmers' flat in the first production of *A Doll's House* was a copy of Raphael's *Sistine Madonna* (c.1512–14), a painting that the Helmers might have encountered on their Italian holiday. This offers a visual image of the perfect woman and mother Nora is expected to be.

A04 **KEY CONNECTION**

Caryl Churchill's play *Cloud Nine* (1979) explores the way the nineteenth century constructed femininity. The downtrodden Victorian wife Betty is played in the first act by a man in a dress. She tells the audience: 'I am a man's creation as you see. And what men want is what I want to be.' This stage picture emphasises the idea of womanhood as a kind of masquerade, just as Nora has to act out Helmer's expectations of what a wife should be and wear the fancy dress in which he chooses to display her.

ACT TWO PART TWO: PAGES 60–4

Summary

- Nora asks Helmer to let Krogstad keep his job; he resists.
- He recalls the faults of her father.
- When she presses him, he sends Krogstad a note of dismissal.
- Helmer promises Nora that he can cope with any consequences.

Analysis

Nora's past

There is a clue in this scene to the Helmers' relationship, dropped so subtly that it is easy to miss. Nora's father was once in danger of losing his job. Helmer, then a lawyer, was sent to investigate and was 'so kind and helpful' (p. 61). Is 'helpful' a **euphemism**? Does it indicate that Helmer concealed some underhand dealing? Notice that Nora does *not* say that Helmer 'proved my father innocent'. If Helmer hid some compromising facts he may have seen Nora as his reward for silence. However, his announcement that he is 'of unassailable reputation' (p. 61) may indicate that he has never consciously articulated this idea, even to himself.

Study focus: A change in language

Note that the **comedy** is sharp here – not for its own sake, but to underline a shift in the way Nora speaks and arguably thinks. Each of Helmer's outbursts about Krogstad is prompted by a stimulus from Nora. These exchanges make us aware that the couple are moving in opposite directions. Nora begins in her usual ingratiating tone, promising 'lots of pretty tricks' (p. 60). But as she questions Helmer's fear of looking unduly influenced by his wife, her argument – why does it matter? – becomes logical. Finally, she uses overtly critical language about Helmer for the first time in the play, calling him 'petty' (p. 62). She may even be laughing at him.

The masculine stereotype

Helmer's pompous self-assurance about his 'strength or courage' (p. 63) is funny. But it also suggests he is trying to live a male stereotype, no more realistic than the ideal woman he wants Nora to be. He does not truly know himself. He is not 'strong' – he collapsed from overwork. He is not even courageous enough to deal with the embarrassment he feels at the presence of Krogstad – whose real sin in Helmer's eyes is not forgery, but reminding him that the class divide between them was once much narrower.

Key quotation: Helmer's snobbery

Helmer complains, '"Torvald this" and "Torvald that" … If he stayed, he'd make my position intolerable.' He wants to deprive a man of his livelihood for using his Christian name (p. 62). This is the most unguarded statement Helmer has made so far. He seems to think it perfectly reasonable and is puzzled by Nora's critical response.

ACT TWO PART THREE: PAGES 64–70

Summary

- Dr Rank tells Nora that he is dying. He says he feels displaced by Mrs Linde.
- They flirt over the silk stockings Nora will wear at the party.
- Nora begins to ask a favour about the money.
- Dr Rank tells her that he loves her. She feels she cannot ask the favour.
- Krogstad arrives. Nora sends Dr Rank to keep Helmer occupied.

Analysis

An adult conversation

For the first time we see a truly adult encounter. It is refreshing after Helmer's relentless infantilising of Nora. The audience are expected to think like adults too. Invalids in nineteenth-century literature often had a special function in the plot. They provided a kind of spiritual dimension. An audience used to sentimental drama might wonder whether Nora would redeem her flaws as a wife through selflessly nursing Rank. Her relief when Rank's bad news turns out to be about his illness indicates that the play will not indulge in such a **cliché**.

A02

Study focus: Subtext

Be aware of **subtext** in this scene: unspoken ideas and emotions pulsing beneath commonplace words and actions. Rank and Nora speak in a code that reveals themselves and their world. First, it makes clear that Nora understands Rank's situation. It also stresses that this is knowledge forbidden to her sex and class. When Nora mentions 'asparagus and *foie gras*' (p. 65) she parrots the kind of lie with which enquiring women were often fobbed off. When he counters it with 'truffles' he indicates his approval of her worldly knowledge. Nora's riposte about 'oysters' – reputedly an aphrodisiac – shows awareness that Rank's father really had syphilis. 'It's too sad that all those lovely things should affect one's spine' brings Rank back to his original complaint that his own spine is paying the price, despite never having 'got any pleasure out of them' (p. 66).

Another mirror image

The discussion of illness develops the theme of heredity, introduced by Helmer's remarks about Nora inheriting her father's extravagance. Rank's role has previously been that of the stock nineteenth-century character the *raisonneur*, the bystander who helps the audience interpret the action. Here, he is another mirror of Nora. Both are victims of corrupt fathers.

Key quotation: Families and retribution **A01**

Dr Rank questions the 'justice' (p. 65) of suffering for the sins of his father. The play rejects the idea of inherited suffering as punishment and explores instead the damage that families do to one another. Nora has *not* inherited her father's attitude to money – but she is suffering for it because it gives Helmer a way to disparage her.

A03 **KEY CONTEXT**

The Russian playwright Anton Chekhov (1860–1904) wrote this famous description of subtext in **naturalistic** drama: 'It is necessary that on the stage everything should be as complex and as simple as in life. People are having dinner, and while they're having it, their future happiness may be decided or their lives may be about to be shattered' (quoted in J. L. Styan's *The Dark Comedy*, 1962, second edition 1968, p. 75). Nora's life reaches a crossroads here, though the scene contains no more remarkable action than a chat in a darkening room.

A03 **KEY CONTEXT**

Knowledge about the causes of sexually-transmitted diseases was hazy in this period. In fact, a child would not inherit syphilis directly from a father, but could be infected if he had infected the mother before she conceived. If aware of this distinction, Ibsen may have chosen to ignore it in order to develop the parallels between Rank and Nora as children betrayed by their fathers and to make it clear that this is an illness that afflicts all levels of society.

The conversation shifts

Nora's reply to Rank changes the conversation. 'Oh yes, that's the saddest thing of all' (p. 66) sounds bland. Rank's response, however, suggests Nora's expression has changed. He searches her face hoping, perhaps, for confirmation that what she really means is 'the saddest part is that therefore we cannot be lovers'. Their retreat into laughter, and her rapid mention of 'Torvald', implies that they are both aware they have just skirted a dangerous corner. Rank's appeal for pity, his fear of being 'forgotten' (p. 66), has an unexpected consequence. Nora slips back into thinking about leaving. This has been on her mind since her conversation with the nurse.

Despite her recent discussion with Mrs Linde, Nora obviously feels that she can ask Rank for money. This may be because she has in her own mind a clear definition of real love. Helmer, she says, would 'never hesitate for an instant to lay down his life for me' (p. 68). But by abandoning **subtext** and speaking plainly, Nora puts love, not sex, back on the agenda. Rank falls gratefully on the opportunity to state that Helmer is not alone in his willingness to sacrifice everything.

Study focus: A decisive moment **A02**

Note Ibsen's method of transcending a stock situation here. The heroine of a popular **well-made play** might face the choice between the villain's unwanted sexual attentions or financial ruin. The audience could enjoy feeling sentimental about her 'fall' or her piety. Here the audience may be in **suspense**, wondering if Nora will compromise herself. This, rather than Krogstad's threats, is the moment of crisis for Nora. It is for the actress to choose exactly how and when she will show Nora reaching her decision not to ask Rank for 'a very great service'. But it is clearly a moment of moral growth. Does Nora's *'slight start'* (p. 68) at Rank's declaration of love indicate her first shocked realisation? Or has she begun earlier in the scene to sense what Rank is going to say? Does she at some point become aware that she is attempting to manipulate her friend for money, just as she has been manipulating her husband?

KEY CONTEXT **A03**

Ibsen's rival and contemporary August Strindberg (1849–1912) summarised this scene as: 'Nora offers herself for sale – to be paid for in cash' (quoted in *Ibsen's Lively Art: A Performance Study of the Major Plays* by Frederick J. Marker and Lise-Lone Marker, 1989, p. 87).

KEY CONTEXT **A03**

St Lucy's Day, the old winter solstice, is a festival of light in Scandinavia. A young woman wearing a crown of lighted candles brings food to the door of each house in her village, and fires are lit to symbolise the breaking of the power of winter. Ibsen taps into this custom to suggest that Nora is a bringer of light in the darkness.

Bringing light

Nora's request for the lamp is a definite change of gear and an example of Ibsen's subtle use of staging. She exploits the new lighting **symbolically**. Saying to Rank, 'Aren't you ashamed of yourself, now that the lamp's been lit?' (p. 69), closes the subject of love definitively. Nora is implying that his declaration belongs to the dark rather than the light of goodness. But because the lamp is real, her tone stays at the level of banter, not reproof. This is a woman who can be gracious and considerate – and who is beginning to make decisions for herself.

Revision task 2: Subtext **A02**

Make notes on Rank and Nora's conversation here, looking carefully at:
- What they communicate through jokes
- What subjects they evade, and how

EXTRACT ANALYSIS: PAGES 66–7

> From 'Be nice now, Dr Rank.' to 'Take that.'

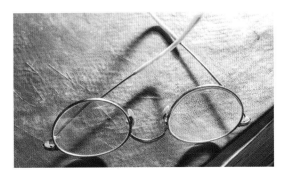

At this point in the conversation Dr Rank may have been trying to decide whether or not Nora is in love with him. He has expressed a little jealousy of Mrs Linde as his possible replacement in Nora's affections. He has also – inadvertently – raised the topic of absence. Nora is contemplating her own absence from the house, by leaving or by suicide.

Nora's flirtatious behaviour with the stockings she will wear at the party shocked its first audience. Ibsen is taking a calculated risk. The audience needs to come close to thinking that Nora will make a crude offer to sleep with Rank – only to understand just how complex the **subtext** really is.

Nora is undeniably taking pleasure in the flirtatious tone. She is cheering herself up after the sad realisation that her friend is dying, by returning to their consciously comic exchanges of a few moments ago. They are, once more, a 'double act', capable of snappy repartee beyond the wit of the other people in their circle. The flirtatiousness also shows Nora's understanding that the dream of a love affair is important to Rank. She knows she is making him happy.

But Nora is also paving the way for her request for money. When she says, 'you'll see how beautifully I shall dance; and you must imagine I'm doing it just for you', she is echoing her promise to 'dance ... in the moonlight' in return for favours from Helmer (p. 61). Her numerous invitations to 'sit down here' and 'Look here!' indicate that Nora is trying to bring Rank physically near her. His ability to identify the stockings as silk may well mean that he is touching them, offering the actors a moment of sensual closeness. The developing darkness Nora mentions creates an atmosphere of intimacy. People tend to speak quietly in the dark. The frankness with which the doctor speaks of his death has opened up the possibility of love between them.

However, their **double entendres** are becoming cruder. Nora's remark about the stockings, 'you can look a bit higher if you want to', is shocking for a respectable wife. In the nineteenth century even to mention underwear would be considered startling. **Paradoxically**, this new crudity means that Nora and Rank also censor themselves. Nora banters with him as if she is already his mistress – but the topic of love has been excluded. Rank's own willingness to join in the game with 'I can't really give you a qualified opinion on that' (implying 'unless you let me see your legs') suggests that he too has decided to use slightly smutty banter to postpone the discourse of love.

Fragile and easily damaged, the stockings are a **metaphor** of this whole encounter. Nora may strike Rank with a stocking, but it is impossible to land a blow with a piece of silk: the effect is more like a kiss. The actors can stress the risqué aspect of this situation, and use it to create camaraderie between Nora and Rank. But they may prefer to make it a moment of tenderness.

ACT TWO PART FOUR: PAGES 70–9

Summary

- Krogstad enters to press his case. He informs Nora that the price of his silence is now a better job at the bank.
- Both of them speak about suicide.
- He drops a letter in the box explaining everything to Helmer, and leaves.
- Mrs Linde arrives, then leaves to try and persuade her former admirer Krogstad to change his mind.
- Nora tries to stop Helmer coming in.
- She distracts him by rehearsing her dance. As Rank accompanies her on the piano, she dances wildly.
- Mrs Linde returns to tell her she cannot find Krogstad. Nora contemplates suicide.

Analysis

Krogstad reveals his feelings

Krogstad's entrance via the back stairs shows a new confidence. Ibsen marks this with costume. In Act One, on legitimate business with Helmer, Krogstad waited politely while the maid took his coat. Here he is in outdoor clothes, suggesting that he has pushed past her. His boots and fur cap make him look larger. They indicate that it is freezing outside, reminding the audience of the darkness and cold into which Nora will step later. Krogstad's language is now far less respectful. Note that his disrespect is largely directed towards Helmer. Krogstad is the only person who expresses outright contempt for him.

This bluntness contrasts with his attitude to Nora, which is far more complex. He does not now remind her that she is a criminal out of malice, but from a sense that they share an experience. He goes further, to suggest that she too may have considered suicide – and is actively '*relieved*' when she says she is not brave enough (p. 72). The previous act showed Krogstad to be more than a stage villain. He now gives an almost **metatheatrical** comment on the crudity of **stock characters** by briskly deflating Nora's image of heroic suicide with a graphic description of her corpse – 'ugly, unrecognizable, hairless' (p. 73). This would shock a nineteenth-century audience. Heroines of popular drama might take their own lives – but tastefully.

Study focus: Using sounds

A02

Note that Krogstad's exit is carefully crafted for **suspense**. The audience is teased with the possibility that he may not leave the letter. Moments later we hear it arrive. The glass front of the mailbox means that Nora can steal glances at the threat until the letter is opened. The use of compromising documents was common in drama, but here it also emphasises that the house is a place of confinement for Nora, both physically and spiritually. Krogstad's noisy footsteps – nobody else walks audibly – are not followed by the sound of the front door closing. It is, in a sense, left 'open' until Helmer locks it in the next act.

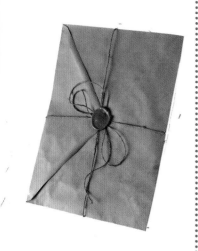

KEY CONTEXT   A03

If you want to explore the differences between Ibsen's characters and the dramatic stereotypes of the day, Jerome K. Jerome's *Stage-Land* (1889) contains an amusing summary of typical stock characters. These include the heroine, the serving girl and, of course, the villain. He points out that: 'The stage villain is superior to the villain of real life. The villain of real life is actuated by mere sordid and selfish motives. The stage villain does villainy, not for any personal advantage to himself, but merely from the love of the thing as an art. Villainy is to him its own reward; he revels in it.' Krogstad, on the other hand, expresses real anger that Helmer has reduced him to the criminal expedient of blackmailing Nora.

Nora's mental state

Nora here speaks of the possibility that 'I should go out of my mind' (p. 74). The idea pervades this act in several different ways. An audience with a taste for the sensational might assume that there is a chance of what nineteenth-century opera called 'the mad scene' – an opportunity for a spectacular emotional display by the heroine. Nora is certainly fragile and afraid at this point – although we know that she is resourceful and practical. But Ibsen has also constructed a character who thinks of *herself* in melodramatic terms: here she has one of her brief **soliloquies**, in which she seems to be acting out just such an emotional display: 'Oh, Torvald, Torvald! Now we're lost!' (p. 74).

Confinement

The talk of keys and closed doors gives a sense of the confinement Nora might expect in an asylum if the fear she expresses were to be realised. This is not all a figment of Nora's melodramatic imagination. Helmer's behaviour is sometimes like that of a jailer. As Nora explains to Mrs Linde, Helmer has the only key to the mailbox. She is not given free access to her own letters. Helmer's apparently joking remark 'Well, may a man enter his own drawing-room again?' (p. 75) shows his disregard for Nora's privacy.

It is also becoming evident that Helmer is impossible to please. First he accuses her of rehearsing her dance too energetically and getting tired; when she tells him she has not rehearsed at all, he snaps, 'Well, you must' (p. 76). While Nora is clearly over-acting her concern about the tarantella to distract Helmer from the mailbox, it is Helmer who provides the description of her state of mind as 'so frightened' and 'helpless' (p. 76) – perhaps thereby encouraging those feelings in her. He is only too happy to accept Nora's invitation to 'Correct me, lead me, the way you always do' (p. 77). Is Nora being sarcastic here? If so, Helmer's obliviousness will be comic – but Nora's sense of being trapped is real.

Study focus: Hysteria **A03**

It is important to be aware here of the potential consequences for Nora of the men's conversation. When Helmer uses the word 'lunacy' (p. 77), and when Dr Rank asks his idiotic question 'she isn't – er – expecting – ?' (p. 78), they are both touching on the notion of female hysteria. This was a common diagnosis of the period for women who exhibited a wide array of symptoms, including nervousness, insomnia, irritability or just a tendency to cause trouble. A woman was considered at risk in girlhood, early marriage, pregnancy, the menopause, old age – in short, all her life. The diagnosis could lead to confinement in an asylum. Helmer and Rank may sound rather foolish, but they have the power to do this.

Revision task 3: Suspense **A02**

This act ends with a **strong curtain**. Ibsen's first audience would be in suspense, wondering how the play would end. List some possible answers from a nineteenth-century perspective. Write about:

- The clues that Ibsen has dropped in the play so far
- The theatrical conventions of the time that might shape their expectations

A05 KEY INTERPRETATION

Norwegian critic Toril Moi suggests that the two men here treat Nora as an object – in fact, a doll: 'Their gaze de-souls her and turns her into a mechanical doll.' (*Henrik Ibsen and the Birth of Modernism*, OUP 2006, p. 239) Moi's analysis of the tarantella is detailed and illuminating.

A05 KEY INTERPRETATION

Alisa Solomon discusses the relationship between theatrical sensationalism for its own sake and Ibsen's more original approach in which Nora herself needs to use theatricality in order to express her feelings. Solomon notes, 'Not a *concession* to the old effect-hunting, Nora's tarantella is an *appropriation* of it.' (*Re-Dressing the Canon: Essays on Theatre and Gender*, Routledge, 1997, p. 55)

EXTRACT ANALYSIS: PAGE 77

> From '*He sits down at the piano.*' to '*You see!*'

Krogstad's letter exposing Nora is in the mailbox. She has no escape now, but is determined to postpone the crisis for one last night. As Helmer insists on reading his letters, she demands that he help her rehearse her dance.

It is credible for Nora to entertain the company with a dance she learned on the Italian holiday. But the meaning of this episode is complex. It is worth noting that this is not an easy dance to perform. Although the tarantella was originally a folk dance, it had been modified in the 1840s to make it a performance piece. It is fast and athletic. We have been informed of Nora's practical skill, but now she also shows herself to be talented.

Ibsen's contemporaries knew the tarantella's origins: its name is derived from *tarantula*. The bite of this spider was thought to cause dance-like convulsions. Though these movements were a symptom of the disease, people believed it could be cured by dancing to sweat the poison out of the system. Nora performs to distract her husband, but she is also choosing to express herself here. We can see the violence of her thoughts about suicide. And a dance linked to poison shows her fear that, as one of the 'constitutional liars' (p. 53) Helmer despises, she is 'poisoning' (p. 54) her children. As people believed they could dance their way to a miraculous recovery, so Nora expects a 'miracle' from Helmer, although it is one she will not allow to happen.

Ibsen's direction that Nora's hair should fall '*over her shoulders*' refers to the **melodramatic** convention that unbound hair implies mental disorder. Nora is acting out her feelings, as she did in her earlier **soliloquy**. But while we watch her dancing theatrically we are also invited to watch her audience. There is an equal focus on the men in Nora's life. We watch them watching her and are aware that neither really understands the intensity of her feelings. Helmer has steadily refused to have a rational discussion about Krogstad. Rank has declared his love at a point when what she needed was practical help. They let her down again here. She becomes, for both men, a spectacle for sexual enjoyment.

They take turns at the piano: Rank's request to 'play for her' suggests he is taking Helmer's place in the only way he can. But while the men discuss her, Nora chooses to speak to the last member of her audience to arrive, Mrs Linde. The claim 'we're having such fun' can be translated more literally as '*watch* the fun'. Nora may feel only another woman can interpret her dance as an expression of pain. When Helmer says that Nora is 'dancing as if your life depended on it', he is being patronising. But when Nora replies 'it does', she is speaking the literal truth as she sees it.

Nora's dance may be undisciplined. But Ibsen also makes it clear that this is *her* dance. She chooses the costume. She does not put on the clothes of the 'fisher-girl' (p. 57). She is refusing to pander to Helmer's taste for exotic foreign costumes and silk stockings, or to his desire to feel socially superior by making her wear the dress of a worker. Instead she wears the dress of the wife and mother she really is. She also chooses the audience. Instead of the neighbours – to whom Helmer wants to show off his beautiful wife like a prized possession – she performs to the people she wants to understand her feelings. Her leap into the centre of the room shows her intent to claim everybody's attention.

This dance does not conform to Helmer's shouted instructions to slow down and be more decorous. Nora ignores the rhythm he conducts. The stage directions here suggest that she may be using the tambourine to insist on beating time as she sees fit. Although she cries 'I must' when Helmer complains that she is dancing too violently, she laughs. She has not laughed at him since she accused him of pettiness over the sacking of Krogstad. Her laughter suggests that the dance is providing her with some degree of emotional release, even if it is not enough to distract Helmer from reading his letter and has to be reinforced by champagne and macaroons. The one thing she is *not* doing in her dance, in fact, is what she said she would do – allow Helmer to instruct her.

When Dr Rank takes over at the piano, Helmer sees it as an opportunity to regain control over Nora and shout instructions. He even moves into an area of the stage we have come to associate with her, near the stove. But it is in vain. Perhaps Rank is encouraging Nora by the speed of his playing; but it is more likely that he is co-operating with the tempo she has chosen. Helmer may well be a comic sight, disgruntled on the edge of the action. He evidently feels so excluded – after all, he is supposed to be the master of the dance – that he virtually orders his guest to stop playing. Given that Helmer gives this order twice, it is likely that Rank too is caught up in the moment.

Helmer's complaint, 'You've forgotten everything I taught you' thus falls into the silence generated by the shock of the sudden end to the tarantella. This allows us a moment to take in the underlying **irony** of his words. Nora is in the process of abandoning most of what she has been taught by Helmer about men, women and morality, as we will discover in the next act.

A05 **KEY INTERPRETATION**

Joseph Losey's 1973 film of *A Doll's House*, freely adapted in places, shows Jane Fonda as Nora dancing the tarantella twice. At home, she performs a kind of cancan. Helmer describes it as a 'wanton display'. In Fonda's interpretation she is, perhaps, trying to seduce him to distract him from the mail. We also see her perform in costume at the party upstairs, a scene that led feminist critics, including Frode Helland, to accuse the director of inviting the audience to be as voyeuristic as the men in the play.

A05 **KEY INTERPRETATION**

The playwright David Edgar points out that part of the power of the tarantella scene comes from the fact that it is a 'social ceremony' that gets out of hand. Performing to guests was common in a world before radio and television and the Helmers' piano suggests that they give musical entertainments regularly. Here, the emotion takes over. (See *How Plays Work*, Nick Hern Books, 2009, p. 147.)

KEY CONNECTION A04

In Charlotte Brontë's *Jane Eyre* (1847), Jane feels compromised by her future husband's insistence on choosing her clothes, which she feels makes him behave like a sultan to his slave: 'He fixed on a rich silk of the most brilliant amethyst dye, and a superb pink satin. I told him ... he might as well buy me a gold gown and a silver bonnet at once.' (Chapter 24) This is the first time we see Nora actually wearing the Capri dress – and she presumably looks uncomfortable because the charming costume has become associated with her husband's possessiveness.

ACT THREE PART ONE: PAGES 80–8

Summary

- Mrs Linde is waiting for the Helmers. Krogstad arrives.
- They talk and renew their old relationship.
- A happy Krogstad decides to take back his letter. But Mrs Linde tells him not to. He goes to wait for her outside.
- Helmer brings Nora home after her dance.
- He tries to make love to her, but they are interrupted by a ring at the door.

Analysis

A slower tempo

The opening of this act teases the audience. The tension has been escalating steadily. They assume that the play will follow the pattern set at the beginning of the previous act, which took up Nora's mounting panic at once. Instead, the curtain rises on Mrs Linde. For a brief moment, Ibsen seems to indulge the audience's desire for tense emotion as she watches anxiously for Krogstad. But on his arrival the audience must accept that they are going to be watching two people quietly discussing their own concerns. This increases the **suspense**. It is also a needful reminder that everybody has a story of their own. Two of the **stock characters** of melodrama– the villain and the **confidante** – are stepping out of their dramatic functions to take the stage in their own right. It is rare to see this pairing – let alone see them developing a genuine and complex relationship.

Study focus: Making an entrance A03

The return of Nora and Helmer shows Ibsen's keen visual sense. He knows the audience is anticipating their arrival and he ensures that it is a spectacular entrance. Their appearance contrasts sharply with the drabness of Mrs Linde. They are both wearing a form of fancy dress. Each of them does so in a way that fits the expectations of society about gender roles. Helmer wears a cloak over ordinary evening clothes. This suggests he wants to give the impression of being above anything so childish as 'dressing up'. Of course, this is in itself a form of 'dressing up' and would make him very conspicuous at a fancy dress dance – perhaps even a talking point. He describes the costume he has chosen for Nora as that of a 'capricious little Capricienne' (p. 85); in other words, he sees her as a changeable child from an alien culture, not part of the 'real' world of money, morality and decision-making.

Helmer taking off Nora's shawl to display her for Mrs Linde's admiration is a significant moment. In Act One Nora spoke proudly to Mrs Linde about saving money by buying cheap dresses. Now, literally dressed by Helmer, she is losing even that small independence.

KEY CONTEXT A03

Note that in this scene Nora is wearing a black shawl over her bright costume, as if death is on her mind. In the previous scene she danced in a multi-coloured shawl over her own dress.

Physical comedy

We have just heard Mrs Linde optimistically telling Krogstad that the truth will help Nora's marriage. However, her attempt to tell Nora this is brought to a quick end by an episode that suggests Helmer and reality are strangers: his hilarious demonstration of how to embroider and knit. This offers an actor with a talent for comedy a piece of **stage business** as interesting as Nora's tarantella: this large man in his evening suit demonstrates how to be a domestic goddess, a **drag act** in miniature.

Helmer would never attempt this if he were not a little drunk – but it is consistent with the way he gives lectures on subjects he knows nothing about. The audience might recall that Nora has earned money from 'fancy work, crocheting, embroidery' (p. 31). She is a professional. Mrs Linde's face as he bustles her out, anxious to avoid walking her home, may contrast comically to her speech as polite employee, calling him 'Mr Helmer' (p. 87).

A love scene with an ugly edge

Ibsen gives the actors considerable freedom about how they play this scene. We have been aware throughout that Helmer desires Nora and at times she seems to enjoy their games and fantasies. Helmer should probably not seem too much of a predator here. The drunkenness – probably not a sensation he is used to – makes him act like an adolescent and voice thoughts he would normally keep to himself. It is **ironic**, however, that the fantasies of this man who persistently lectures his wife about truthfulness are all about secrecy. And, although he may not have talked about them, he regularly indulges in them in a way that might be socially awkward for Nora. He remains 'aloof' (p. 88) from her in company, so he can imagine she is his secret mistress.

Having enjoyed narrating the fantasy, Helmer has such a clear image in his head of Nora as reluctant young bride that he misses her anxiety and exhaustion. He completely fails to catch the critical edge to her voice when she says, 'I know you never think of anything but me' (p. 88). The *real* Nora is invisible to him, until she breaks the fantasy by refusing sex. This is, perhaps, the first time she has ever asserted herself like this, and the first time in the play he has said anything as potentially violent as 'Don't want, don't want – ? Aren't I your husband?' (p. 88) The marriage appears to be reaching a crisis point before any of Krogstad's revelations.

 A03 KEY CONTEXT

In Ibsen's play *Pillars of Society*, a female character says, 'This society of yours is a bachelors' club. You don't see women.' Helmer sees the Nora he wants to see.

A01 PROGRESS BOOSTER

It is always helpful to look at any directions the playwright gives about clothing. Throughout *A Doll's House* we learn about characters' financial situations, their tastes and their access to the wider world through their choice of garments. It is a good idea to makes notes about what the main characters are wearing in each scene.

Key quotation: Nora and irony **A01**

Until now Nora's flattery of Helmer may have been insincere, but here her tone seems blatantly ironic. When she comments 'You're always right, whatever you do' (p. 87) she has just witnessed Helmer's rudeness to Mrs Linde.

EXTRACT ANALYSIS: PAGES 80–4

> From 'Well, Krogstad' to 'I've never been so happy in my life before!'

The previous act has ended with a frantic Nora telling herself she has just thirty-one hours to live. As the curtain rises, we assume she is in the flat above at the party. At first sight Mrs Linde's presence is a disappointment, a device to prolong suspense and prepare for Nora's entrance. When Krogstad arrives, the audience assumes that they will have the conversation about Nora that Mrs Linde had hoped to have at his house. The first surprise comes when he bitterly complains about 'the old story ... a woman chucking a man because something better turns up' (p. 81). Although we know that he has had a relationship with Mrs Linde, we have not expected it to be important to him now. Ibsen is making it very clear that none of his characters is simply there for the convenience of the central story.

This scene will be the culmination of all the scenes in which Nora has been faced with 'mirrors' of herself. Here, two characters who share aspects of her experience and situation confront not Nora, but each other. And in the process they are radically changed. Mrs Linde and Krogstad foreshadow the discussion between Helmer and Nora at the end of the play, even in their position on the stage. This scene can be usefully read alongside the final episode – although the choices these 'mirrors' make will be very different.

We have already seen independent Mrs Linde as a possible model for Nora, though there is such a contrast between her weary poverty and Nora's lively health. However, it is now plain that their experience of life has been quite similar. Helmer provided Nora's father with vital (possibly less than legal) 'help' to save his job – and was awarded Nora as a sort of prize. Mrs Linde made a deliberate choice to take a husband who would provide for her family. Nora has had better luck in purely material terms – Mrs Linde's husband went bankrupt and left her struggling for years. But the women share the experience of **commodification –** of being sold. Both have had their circumstances decided by corrupt and inadequate men. Marriage was the only possible way to help their families. Only Mrs Linde has so far reached an understanding of her situation. Only Mrs Linde knows what life is like as someone who refuses to be commodified. The choices that she makes in this scene are those of a free and independent woman. As she tells Krogstad, 'a woman who has sold herself once for the sake of others doesn't make the same mistake again.' (p. 83) Whether Nora will mirror this aspect of her remains to be seen – although her decision not to ask Dr Rank for money suggests that she will.

Krogstad has repeatedly insisted on his likeness to Nora as a fellow forger. He now becomes a mirror of her situation in a more poignant way. He reminds Mrs Linde 'what people think of me here' (p. 82); he is a man with a ruined reputation – the fate he has wished on Nora. When he realises he has a chance to recover, he also wishes a similar redemption for her.

The characters are anchored at the table for most of this episode, which places them on an equal footing. Previously the space has tended to underline differences in the power of the sexes. Nora has moved around both Helmer and Rank, embracing, dancing and playing on their physical closeness. This neutral arrangement foreshadows their sober settling of accounts. Yet this is also a love scene, and a highly original one. Unusually for the period, a woman is the active party. Mrs Linde has chosen the setting, by coming to town to find Krogstad. She is the one who defines the nature of the relationship she wants. Rather than just longing to be loved, she hopes for an active role. She wants someone to 'work for' (p. 82) and children 'to be a mother to' (p. 83).

Significantly, too, Mrs Linde has thought out the kind of language that suits such a love, and defined its moral basis. She is clear that her offer to care for Krogstad is not the **rhetoric** of 'self-sacrifice' that leads Nora to contemplate suicide. She has all the information about Krogstad's past but she assumes that love has the power to motivate change; she believes it can transform him into 'a different person'. Picking up Krogstad's image of 'a shipwrecked man clinging to a spar' (p. 82), she offers a straightforwardly practical image of them joining hands.

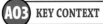

A03 **KEY CONTEXT**

Ibsen found in this scene the germ of a later play, *When We Dead Awaken* (1899). Here two people with a difficult experience of relationships come together, like Nils Krogstad and Mrs Linde, to 'stitch our tattered lives together'. As the characters no longer had such a key role in shaping the plot, he could focus more clearly on their emotional development. However, this meant he could not use one of the most effective surprises in *A Doll's House*. The audience would assume that when Krogstad and Mrs Linde found happiness they would destroy the letter. Instead, they let it do its work from more kindly motives.

Krogstad's approach, too, is unromantic. He first assumes that Mrs Linde cannot be fully aware of his crime, then that she is chiefly motivated by care for Nora. It takes time for him to believe that he can be valued. When he does, it is enough to make him say, as he leaves, 'I've never been so happy in my life before!' (p. 84). Nora will be standing on the identical spot on the stage when she speaks at the end of the play about 'the miracle of miracles' (p. 104) – by which she means a genuine marriage of equals. Krogstad's line ensures that we will think back to this alliance of two people learning from past mistakes to attempt such a thing.

One reason that they have a chance of achieving it is that they start by acknowledging the weak and fallible people they have been, rather than from idealised notions about what a man and a woman ought to be. This flawed, tentative but hopeful couple are at once a guarantee that partnership is possible, and a lesson as to how much it costs emotionally to make this journey.

ACT THREE PART TWO: PAGES 88–94

Summary

- Dr Rank calls to see Nora. She asks about his latest test and he reveals his death is certain.
- He leaves after a final goodbye.
- Helmer opens the mailbox, noting the lock has been forced. He finds Rank's cards.
- He still presses Nora to make love, but she tells him to read his letters.
- Helmer is enraged at Krogstad's letter.

Analysis

Private language

A moment ago it seemed inevitable that Helmer's insistence would trigger a final confrontation– although a nineteenth-century audience might wonder, in their tightly censored theatre, how this scene could possibly continue. Instead, there is another teasing postponement, which rapidly proves to be one of the most extraordinary sequences in the play. Helmer's greeting is rude and sarcastic. Rank's response, though blandly polite – 'I thought I heard your voice' (p. 88) – makes it uncomfortably clear he has heard Helmer pestering Nora, and her angry and scared reaction.

This is a dark and very modern **comedy** of embarrassment. Nora's remarks about champagne and high spirits draw Rank into an alliance against Helmer. Their private code is still outwardly frivolous but is now charged with sadness. Helmer adds a further dimension. His silly remarks – 'Scientific experiment! Those are big words for my little Nora to use!' (p. 89) – are initially a source of amusement, to us, and also to Rank and Nora. He is the butt of their private joke, trapped between them in a reverse image of the tarantella scene where Nora was the object of the men's gaze. As the scene goes on, Rank understands just how deeply Helmer undervalues Nora. He cuts Helmer's remark about the problems of conveying 'The Spirit of Happiness' with the sharp retort, 'Your wife need only appear as her normal, everyday self – ' (p. 90).

A03

Study focus: Symbolic fire

Note how Nora's gesture of lighting the cigar takes on a ritual quality. She is making a special effort to perform a courtesy that would more conventionally be done by Helmer, aware that this is a goodbye. Rank shows that he too is aware of the symbolism with 'thank you for the light' (p. 90). It recalls how she put an end to his declaration of love by ordering the lamp. Perhaps he is glad he has not betrayed his friend Helmer in his last days. The phrase also connotes truth and virtue in more general terms – and the idea that Nora 'lights up' Rank's life. In this context the word can also be translated as 'fire' with all its overtones of warmth and passion: these shades of meaning will be present through the sight of the flame she carries.

Nora's mixed feelings

Helmer's desire to 'offer my life and my blood, everything' (p. 92) springs from drunkenness and selfish pleasure that Rank is now out of the picture. But although he is barely aware of what he is saying – he is still trying to make love to her – it is a crucial moment for Nora. Her **body language** and expression as she insists that he read his letters are important. Helmer has just confirmed that she can expect a 'miracle' of noble sacrifice from him. At the same time, however, his manner, and his callous attitude to Rank, have brought her close to despising him. The jagged rhythm of her **soliloquy** on suicide shows how painful her feelings are. Her instinctive choice of Helmer's garment to wrap around her suggests that she still longs for his protection. But the phrases themselves are **clichés**. The shawl over her head is the standard wear for a heroine of **melodrama** cast out of her home on a stormy night. It is as if Nora is forcing herself against all reason to take Helmer's heroics at face value. If he will be a noble hero, she must be the noble heroine, even if that means death.

Helmer places the blame

As Helmer emerges from his study, the stage picture mirrors the beginning of Act One when he popped out to reprove his 'little squanderbird' (p. 24). One of the cruellest **ironies** of the scene is his description of Nora's behaviour as 'the weakness of a woman' (p. 94). Weakness is exactly what he has wanted from Nora. By locking the door and proclaiming, 'You're going to stay here and explain yourself' (p. 93), he underlines his part in confining her to the 'doll's house' and making her a child-wife. In this scene Helmer endlessly repeats the word 'I'. Even while he imagines his fate is punishment for his own most serious error – helping Nora's father – he manages to blame Nora: 'I did it for your sake. And now you reward me like this' (p. 93).

A03 **KEY CONTEXT**

The careful arrangement of the characters to remind us of the tarantella scene in Act Two reflects Ibsen's growing stagecraft. He was keen to reform the 'staginess' of the Kristiania Theatre and told the actors that 'Groupings and positioning must be given the necessary thought...the positions vis-à-vis each other to change as often as is natural; in general, every scene and every tableau ought as far as possible to reflect reality.' (Robert Ferguson, *Henrik Ibsen*, Richard Cohen Books, London, 1996, p. 229)

A theatrical couple

Helmer fails to realise that Nora intends to take responsibility for her action and take her own life. His sneer at her for being 'melodramatic' (p. 94) is ironic in the light of his false heroics just a few lines previously. The only future he can imagine is *all* 'acting'. Nora will continue playing the loving wife to save his reputation. By making Helmer use the word 'melodramatic' for the first time in the play, the text stresses to its nineteenth-century audience that the simplistic moral codes of the old theatre are being tested to destruction. Nora and Helmer themselves have often used the language of melodrama. It has been difficult for them to find a vocabulary to express their deepest feelings that does not rely on the sexual stereotypes of sentimental drama. This reliance on gender clichés is the real weakness of their relationship – although it has also, perhaps, kept them together.

A05 **KEY INTERPRETATION**

In Patrick Garland's 1973 film of *A Doll's House*, Helmer (played by Anthony Hopkins) strikes Claire Bloom's Nora when he has read the letter. The bruise is visible for the rest of the film. Ibsen's stage directions never call for violence, but there is a strong undercurrent of rage in Helmer's lines. You may find it clarifies your understanding of the play to decide how you would choose to stage a sequence like this.

Key quotation: Helmer's feelings **A01**

Helmer dismisses Rank with, 'His suffering and loneliness seemed to provide a kind of dark background to the happy sunlight of our marriage.' (p. 91) The possessiveness implied by such language is the polar opposite of Rank and Nora's goodbye expressing mutual care.

ACT THREE PART THREE: PAGES 94–104

Summary

- A letter arrives from Krogstad returning the document with the forged signature.
- Helmer rejoices that he is saved, but ignores his wife.
- He goes on to forgive her at great length, while she changes her clothes.
- Nora emerges in everyday dress and says that she is leaving him.

Analysis

A very original stage picture

Ibsen's stagecraft is striking here. Every **well-made play** of the period involved compromising documents – a letter, a will. The playwright might contrive a situation where a letter lies on a table for a whole act like a ticking time bomb. Here, the compromising paper gains its most sinister significance by *ceasing* to be a threat. Krogstad's change of heart ought to mean a happy ending with the characters clustering in a cheerful group for the final curtain. Instead we see the half-dressed and obviously puzzled maid. Dragged out of bed in the middle of the night, she is trying to do her job and give the note to Nora. Helmer stops her, not caring that his wife is humiliated in front of the servant. He then appears to slam the door in the maid's face in his eagerness to grab the letter.

Helmer's focus

It is worth noting that Krogstad writes to Nora, rather than his employer. She is evidently the person he respects more. Not only does Helmer interpret the letter as *his* salvation rather than Nora's, he has no interest in Krogstad. He does not even speak his name. Even though Krogstad's change of heart has taken place in his own living room, even though Krogstad and Mrs Linde are both his employees, he is only interested in what affects him. The whole episode, for Helmer, proves that people behave according to the stereotypes of **melodrama** – the silly wife, the noble husband, and the minor character whose motives are of no interest. Unconsciously, Helmer seems to be denying that individuals can change. By throwing Krogstad's note on the fire he is burning the evidence that change happens.

Clinging to the stereotype

Helmer's long speech on forgiveness is an attempt to recover a position he has lost by his selfishness of the last few minutes. You might ask what, exactly, he is forgiving, since Nora's action has not harmed him and its motive was to do him good. For Helmer, though, the attraction lies in the power that it gives him. It makes him both her husband and her father. But both of these men have profoundly betrayed her: her father has effectively sold her, her husband has disowned her. Meanwhile, she has been Helmer's protector, shielding him from painful facts (even from the sight of knitting), has saved his life and been genuinely ready to sacrifice her own.

 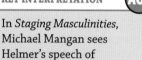

A02

Anticipation

Helmer's speech allows the actress time to take off 'my fancy-dress' (p. 96) It also gives the audience a challenging space to consider what they want to see next. Many of Ibsen's first audience would have expected a meek entrance in nightwear by a wife prepared to confine herself still more closely in the home. Modern audiences, listening to Helmer, hope this will not happen.

Study focus: Nora's logic

Note how the 'reckoning' at the table is structured with great care. Points are raised and discussed almost as if we are in the courtroom where Helmer once worked. The arguments move from the house itself to the wider world. It begins with Nora's domestic unhappiness. Helmer hopes to change that by changing *her* with an 'education' he imagines he can deliver. Then it moves to the political: Helmer appeals to all aspects of male **hegemony**: public opinion, **patriarchy**, the Church, the Law. Nora counters this by asserting the right of the individual to question them. Then – after one last attempt by Helmer at heroic generalisation about what men do – the conversation returns to the personal. But this time the subject is Helmer himself. Still unable to grasp that he needs to change as much as Nora, he tries to suggest what 'we' might do.

Mutual suffering

This slow but inexorable dismantling of the relationship makes a solid frame for a scene of emotional intensity. Both characters are in pain. Nora and Helmer have done their best within their limited understanding of love. While Nora now wants to redefine love, she is not trying to punish the man who has done her a 'great wrong' (p. 97). She accepts responsibility for the 'tricks' (p. 98). But she has already taken off her fancy dress while Helmer is still 'dressed up' as the master. It will be more difficult for him to abandon his illusions, simply because society will be on his side.

A famous exit

As the scene moves to its close, Helmer is more and more physically isolated in the doll's house. Finally it is 'Empty!' and all he has left is the idea of a 'miracle' (p. 104). In Ibsen's first draft Helmer cried, 'I believe in them.' In the final draft he cries, 'I want to believe in them' (Egil Törnqvist, *A Doll's House*, 1995, pp. 39–40). What he has to believe is that he and Nora can become individuals capable of moral choice. Ibsen's wording does not suggest optimism. However, Helmer is alone, talking to himself as Nora did at her first entrance. At that point it suggested loneliness, and it does now. But it was only alone that Nora was able to set out on her journey to independence.

Revision task 4: The final curtain

A05

Ibsen was obliged to write a different ending for the play in which Nora stays for the sake of the children. Make notes on how you think this might work. Write about:

- Whether this might be dramatically effective
- Whether a different ending would strengthen or weaken the central arguments

---

A03 KEY CONTEXT

One way to understand the shock caused by the ending of the play is to look at the many parodies of Ibsen that resulted. One of the liveliest was by the Scottish playwright James Barrie, which opens with a woman recalling, 'To run away from my second husband just as I ran away from my first, it feels quite like old times.' Barrie called it, 'A parody of the greatest craftsman that ever wrote.' (*Barrie: the Definitive Edition of the Plays*, Hodder and Stoughton 1948, p. 5)

A03 KEY CONTEXT

Ibsen was forced to change the ending for the first German production of *A Doll's House*. In this version Helmer confronts Nora with her sleeping children:

HELMER Tomorrow, when they wake and call for their mother, they will be... motherless!

NORA (*trembling*) Motherless!

HELMER As you once were.

NORA Motherless! (*After an inner struggle she lets her bag fall and says:*) Ah, though it is a sin against myself, I cannot leave them. (*She sinks almost to the ground by the door*)

PROGRESS CHECK

Section One: Check your understanding

These tasks will help you to evaluate your knowledge and skills level in this particular area.

1. What do we learn about Nora and Helmer from looking at their home? Make a list of key items on the stage and suggest their significance.

2. What things has Nora bought, and what happens to them? Make brief notes on each.

3. What visitors come to the house, and how are they received? Write a short note on each.

4. What differences do you notice in Nora when Helmer is not present?

5. What games does Nora play with Helmer and why? Write a list and suggest a possible motive for each.

6. How many characters in the play have secrets? Make a list and suggest what might happen if each secret were discovered.

7. What happens to the paper with the forged signature before and during the play? Make brief notes in chronological order.

8. How many people in the play have a soliloquy? What do they talk about? Write a short note on each.

9. What do we learn about Nora's early life? Make brief notes on each event.

10. What does Nora's Neapolitan outfit mean to the characters who handle it or see her wear it? Write notes on each.

11. What do we know about the Helmers' servants? Write notes on each one.

12. There are a number of doors on the set. Write notes on each one that is mentioned and say where it leads, and how it is used in the play.

13. How does Nora raise the money to pay off the loan? What difficulties does she encounter in doing so? Write brief notes in chronological order.

14. How many times does Nora change her clothes, and why? Write your ideas in a two-column table.

15. What subjects does Nora discuss with Dr Rank without Helmer's knowledge? Write a brief note on each saying why she does not talk to Helmer about each one.

16. What do we know about the relationship between Krogstad and Mrs Linde? Make brief notes.

17. Examine the time frame of the play. Make a two-column table for each act, showing the main events and the time of day they take place.

18. Nora feels the men in her life have failed her. List her main reasons in the case of Helmer, Rank and her late father.

19. What happens to the Christmas tree? Write short notes on its appearance in each act, explaining what this adds to the play.

20. How do the other characters in the play describe Nora? Write down two or three quotations for each character.

Section Two: Working towards the exam

Below are five tasks which require longer, more developed answers. In each case, read the question carefully, select the key areas you need to address, and plan an essay of six to seven points. Write a first draft, giving yourself an hour to do so. Make sure you include supporting evidence for each point, including quotations.

1. Explore the function of clothing in the play.
2. Helmer uses the word 'melodrama' about Nora. Which characters do you consider to behave melodramatically, and why?
3. 'The subplot is simply a device to prolong the suspense.' Do you agree?
4. Examine the role of money in the play.
5. 'The change we see in Nora in the final scene is too rapid to be believable.' Do you agree?

Progress check	1	2	3	4	5
(rate your understanding on a level of 1–low, to 5–high)					
The significance of particular events and how they relate to each other					
How the major and minor characters contribute to the action					
How Ibsen uses the device of subtext					
How Ibsen structures the play					
The final outcome of the story and how this affects our view of the protagonists					

CHARACTERS

Torvald Helmer, *Nora's husband*

Nora Helmer

Ivor, Bobby and Emmy, *Nora and Torvald's children*

Dr Rank, *a family friend*

Nils Krogstad, *Torvald's employee*

Christine Linde, *Nora's friend*

Anne-Marie, *the nurse*

Helen, *the maid*

Characterisation

Progress booster: A new approach

It is important to remember that 'character', in the nineteenth century, generally meant something unchangeable. You were born with certain traits and you expressed them throughout your whole life. In the popular theatre 'characters' were defined rigidly: young girls were sweet and innocent, villains were bad to the bone. The study of 'character' meant making a list of specific qualities.

The **naturalistic** theatre worked differently. Ibsen and his successors were aware that people might change and grow. *A Doll's House* works on the assumption that people can say one thing and then express the opposite point of view, as Nora does about Helmer's feelings for her in the future in Act One. This is not because Ibsen saw people as liars, but because he realised they do not always understand themselves. He understood that people acquired their opinions, their personal style and even emotions from a whole range of sources – parents, the Church, popular fiction.

A03 **KEY CONTEXT**

The playwright and novelist John Galsworthy (1867–1933) wrote plays in the 1920s which were greatly influenced by Ibsen. He commented that 'a human being is the best plot there is ... the dramatist who hangs his characters to his plot, instead of hanging plot to his characters, is guilty of cardinal sin.' (Quoted in Eric Bentley, *The Life of the Drama*, Methuen 1965, p. 55) In *A Doll's House*, this priority explains the care Ibsen devotes to Krogstad, who could have the same function in the play as a far less complex character.

Creating characters

It took Ibsen twelve months to plan *A Doll's House*. He talked about it as a process of becoming closely acquainted with his characters. Writing the first draft was like meeting them during a railway journey and chatting with them. The second draft was like 'a month spent with them at a spa … I may still be wrong about certain essentials'; the third draft made them 'intimate friends' (quoted in Clurman, *Ibsen*, 1977, p. 22). At one time Ibsen had wanted to be a painter, and he imagined his characters with a painter's visual flair. He once complained that an actress playing Nora had the wrong kind of hands.

The actor and the character

Ibsen spent years working closely with actors. This taught him to value their contribution to creating a character on stage. You can understand through reading that even trivial remarks and simple actions in the play can 'say' a great deal that is never spoken aloud. However, it is the job of the actor to decide exactly how and when to show this to the audience. In his own lifetime Ibsen saw one Nora dance the tarantella with passion and another with numb exhaustion. He saw one Helmer in late middle age and another who was young and handsome but as pompous as an old man.

All the characters are vehicles for experienced actors. They are not recipes to follow to the letter, but opportunities to make choices. How a character is played, and how the audience understands that character, will depend on the circumstances in which these choices are made. The cultural climate and the political, social or geographical setting will bring about different readings. All of them will offer something new to their audiences and bring Ibsen's pages to life in a new way.

A05 **KEY INTERPRETATION**

The playwright David Edgar explains one important principle of character creation: 'In drama we are not seeing ordinary people engaging in the regular business of everyday life, which is, of course, the habitual. We are seeing people in exceptional circumstances, and thus we are seeing them behaving uncharacteristically.' (*How Plays Work*, Nick Hern Books, 2009, p. 51) Krogstad's decision to blackmail Nora pressurises her into a process of radical action and rapid change.

Nora Helmer

Who is Nora Helmer?

- Nora is the wife of Torvald Helmer and the mother of three children. She saved his life by borrowing money to pay for his convalescence, and is now secretly working to repay it.

- The moneylender, Krogstad, is blackmailing her as she forged a signature to get the money.

- When her husband shows he is willing to let her bear the consequences alone, she is disillusioned and leaves him.

A star role

Nora is one of the longest and most complex female dramatic roles. Ibsen's early audiences found her difficult to understand. They expected figures on stage to be consistent. It was rare for any character to take charge of their own growth. It was even rarer for a woman to do so. The change from the flighty girl of Act One to the sober figure seated at the table in Act Three seemed incredible. (As recently as 1977 the director Harold Clurman admitted that for a long time he had seen the rapid change in Nora as a flaw in the play.) Throughout the action, however, we see latent strengths in Nora. The energy of the play lies in her discovery of this strength.

An active character

Ibsen rapidly establishes Nora as someone with a zest for life. She takes pleasure in the Christmas tree. She enjoys macaroons and champagne. She is physically expressive. We see her touching and kissing Helmer affectionately. She plays enthusiastically with her children, crawling under the table to play hide-and-seek. (Given the restrictions of nineteenth-century clothing for women, this suggests she is quite athletic.) Her instinct is to reach out to people. We see her embrace the nurse, Mrs Linde and Dr Rank. She also has a natural democracy. Nora's admission that she enjoyed the talk of the servants in her father's house contrasts with Helmer's bluster about Krogstad's use of Christian names. All this endears her to the audience. It also means that she is constantly seen in motion. This physical vitality suggests that she has the energy to sustain the very difficult inner journey she undertakes.

Nora as actor

Nora's tarantella shows the instincts of a natural performer. Dance lets her express what she cannot say. It confirms what we have already begun to realise: Nora is becoming aware of 'performing' the role of wife which society has scripted for her. The Nora perkily acting out the role of 'skylark' or 'squirrel' in Act One may enjoy the game. She may enjoy the power she has to wheedle money from Helmer by *playing with his coat buttons'* (Act One, p. 26). Nevertheless she knows that this kind of power will be gone *'when I'm no longer pretty'* (Act One, p. 36). At some point she may feel resentment at the *'tricks'* (Act Two, p. 60) she performs in order to ask Helmer for anything. After all, her problems are the result of his stubborn refusal to look after his health.

KEY INTERPRETATION **A05**

Ibsen's biographer Robert Ferguson considers the ending to be flawed: 'Dramatically it is necessary. Psychologically it is not. Nora has already proved herself the stronger.' (Robert Ferguson, *Henrik Ibsen*, Richard Cohen Books, 1996, p. 245)

KEY INTERPRETATION **A05**

Geraldine Cousin's book *Women in Dramatic Place and Time* pays tribute to the central place of *A Doll's House* in the feminist imagination: 'With Nora, at the commencement of her journey, are, potentially, so many other women, and, though the terrain of Nora's future remains unknown, she is the prototype of later travellers.' (Routledge, 1996, p. 1)

Study focus: The actor as Nora

Note the choices available to the actor deciding how and when to show Nora's first signs of discontent. Perhaps her conversation with Mrs Linde, when Nora expresses her pleasure in 'working and earning money … almost like being a man' (Act One, p. 37), makes Nora feel differently about the way that, only moments later, she flatters and persuades to get her friend a job at the bank. The actress could choose to show such feelings through her facial expression.

On the other hand, she might prefer to express Nora's disquiet later, in the scene where she tries to introduce the topic of Krogstad while requesting help with her fancy dress. Ibsen is careful to arrange the scene so that Nora's **body language** and facial expression are unseen by Helmer as she dresses the Christmas tree. As well as showing the fear and stress she is experiencing, she may indicate that she actively resents and dislikes playing the part of a silly, helpless wife who 'can't get anywhere' (p. 53) without the help of a husband. However and whenever the actor may choose to make it fully clear to us, Nora certainly reaches a point where her feelings and her outward behaviour contradict each other.

Conscience or convention?

Ibsen's first jottings towards the play indicate that he was interested in the idea of 'two kinds of conscience, one for men and one, quite different, for women' (Michael Meyer, *Ibsen*, 1985, p. 321). Helmer is governed by the rules of society and Nora habitually follows her heart. You could argue that, at the beginning of the play, neither of them has a genuine 'conscience' at all. They are not rational and ethical human beings but creatures of convention.

Ibsen gives us the details we need to understand Nora's background. He shows that some of her less attractive qualities are products of her upbringing and its limitations. Her naïveté in assuming that the law will 'understand' her **motivation** perhaps comes from her father, who was capable of dubious behaviour. Her snobbish attitude to Krogstad reflects Helmer's own. Her smug refusal to consider the problems of 'strangers' (Act One, p. 25) stems from an ignorance of the world which Helmer is only too keen to encourage, pushing away worldly friends like Dr Rank. By the end of the play, Nora is actively interested in 'strangers' and intends to do something about her ignorance. She is not only aware that she knows nothing beyond the 'play-room' (Act Three, p. 98), she is well aware that her father and husband have kept her there.

Determined to change

By the end of the play, Nora is aware that her personality has been largely put together by men – the two men who love her, and, behind them, a whole spectrum of masculine authority from the Law to the Church. They have treated her like an object, to be played with or looked at or sold.

A03 **KEY CONTEXT**

A Doll's House has often been staged with a clear political intent, and such productions centre on the character of Nora. In the 1920s *A Doll's House* was banned in China. Jiang Qing (1914–91), later the third wife of Mao Zedong, was an advocate of rights for women – such as the right not to have their feet bound when young – and made her name as Nora in a 1935 production, seen as the beginning of cultural modernity in China.

KEY CONTEXT   (A03)

When Ibsen began to insist on his original ending, some theatres chose to create their own. In one version in Berlin, Helmer arrives at the house of Krogstad and Mrs Linde to find Nora. She whispers, 'Have you then truly forgiven me?' He produces a large bag of macaroons, and she cries 'The miracle of miracles!' (Robert Ferguson, *Henrik Ibsen*, Richard Cohen Books, 1996, p. 245)

KEY CONTEXT   (A03)

One of the most hostile of Ibsen's early critics in England was Clement Scott of the *Daily Telegraph*. After seeing *A Doll's House* he coined the word 'Ibsenite' to denote 'an unlovely, selfish creed' of individualism (*Theatre*, July 1889). When he saw a club production of Ibsen's banned play *Ghosts*, dealing with sexually-transmitted disease, he went on to say that 'Ibsenite' signified 'gross, and almost putrid indecorum' (*Daily Telegraph*, 14 March 1891). Nora arguably *does* become an individual in her own right at the end of the play. Scott seems to feel that this was in itself a selfish choice for a woman.

In order to become a subject rather than an object Nora must shape a new self. Her plans have the same clear-sightedness as her farewell to Dr Rank. She replaces her fantasies of herself as a noble suicide and Helmer as the heroic miracle-worker with modest expectations. Her decision to stay the night with Mrs Linde implies that she does not expect her life to be better than that of her old school friend. She intends to work. This is realistic, as she is an experienced copyist and knows exactly what a woman can earn.

Nora is also profoundly aware of the emotional costs of what she is doing. The break with her children has already begun; although she is no longer haunted by the idea (planted by Helmer) that she might corrupt them, she does feel that she cannot 'educate' them properly (p. 99). She also considers that neither she nor Helmer feels real love for the other. She pays tribute to his kindness. She admits that she will 'often think of' him (p. 104). Her wry response to his suggestion that they could live as brother and sister – 'You know quite well that that wouldn't last' – hints that she still desires him (p.103). For the first time, however, she talks about 'duty' (p. 100) rather than about love; she has become a person with a considered moral code, a 'conscience', rather than simply loving instincts. Helmer, meanwhile, can only repeat the same old patronising **clichés**. Ibsen seems to be suggesting that if the 'consciences' of the sexes are different, the female conscience is more developed.

Nora the light giver

At the start of the play Nora frequently gravitates to the warmth and safety of the stove. When faced by Dr Rank's declaration of love and the temptation to exploit it for money, she demands light. In the last act, offering kindness to a dying man, she is herself a giver of light. Ibsen once remarked to a woman who likened herself to Nora because

she had run away with her lover: 'My Nora went alone.' It is Nora's unflinching solitude at the end of the play that marks her, with all her faults, as a heroine unique in her century.

Revision task 5: What does Nora want?   (A02)

Actors in a **naturalistic** drama often begin from the idea that each character has specific desires, and that everything they do is an attempt to gain them. Write about:

● What Nora wants in her first scene with Helmer

● What she wants in the last scene of the play

Key quotation: Nora's relationships   (A02)

Nora is already aware that 'there are some people whom one loves, and others whom it's almost more fun to be with' (Act Two, p. 69). Although Nora comes late to the conclusion that she does not love Helmer, she does know that she has the capacity to sustain many different kinds of relationship.

Torvald Helmer

Who is Torvald Helmer?

- He is Nora's husband, a former lawyer, who now has a new post at the bank.
- He collapsed from overwork and does not know that Nora paid for his cure.
- Terrified of debt, he discovers that Nora has forged a signature to get money.
- Both the Helmers are blackmailed by the moneylender, the bank clerk Krogstad.
- When Krogstad relents, Helmer tries to restore his relationship with Nora, but she no longer loves him and leaves him.

A good match

It is difficult for a twenty-first-century audience to appreciate that, as nineteenth-century husbands go, Helmer is not a bad prospect. Even when leaving, Nora says, 'you've always been so kind to me' (Act Three, p. 101). He is industrious to a fault, overworking himself sick to achieve promotion and provide for his family. He is gentle. Marital violence was not illegal at the time, but Helmer never hurts Nora even when furious. He likes luxuries, but does not over-indulge – his tipsiness on the party champagne suggests that he is not normally a drinker.

Money and obsession

Helmer's horror of debt seems neurotic. His lecture to Nora – 'Suppose I were to borrow fifty pounds today, and you spent it all over Christmas, and then on New Year's Eve a tile fell off a roof on to my head' (Act One, p. 24) – may be playful exaggeration, but this carefully painted picture suggests he broods on the possibility. Debt anxiety was rife in the nineteenth century. In spite of this Helmer can be generous. Nora seems genuinely pleased with the money he gives her for Christmas shopping, and he relishes surprising her with 'something up my sleeve to hang in gold paper on the Christmas tree' (Act One, p. 54).

A loving husband

Helmer believes that he loves Nora, and says that he and her father 'loved you more than anyone in the world' (Act Three, p. 97). He is furious that she has ruined his reputation, and plans to keep the children from her and preserve only the shell of a marriage. But he cannot quite manage to say he no longer cares. Nora is 'someone I once loved so dearly – and whom I still – !' (Act Three, p. 94). His repeated allusions to songbirds and squirrels, together with Nora's promise to 'turn myself into a little fairy and dance for you in the moonlight' (Act Two, p. 61), suggest that he often shows sexual desire in a playful spirit.

Jealousy

He is also jealous and insensitive. He enjoys the fantasy of Nora as his new bride, pursuing it even after hearing of Dr Rank's imminent death. He enjoys showing off Nora's beauty – 'worth looking at, don't you think?' (Act Three, p. 85) – but once she has been admired he has little interest in other people. Nora tells Mrs Linde he wants to 'have me all to himself' (Act Two, p. 58) and that he refuses to let her talk about old friends. When Rank is dying, Helmer comments it is good now that 'we only have each other' (Act Three, p. 92).

A03 KEY CONTEXT

The name 'Torvald' derives from the Old Norse words *thor* and *valdr*, 'thunder-god' and 'rule' – a name that suggests both heroism and bluster. Nora usually addresses him by this name, although it would be more common for a wife to use his surname. Does this suggest childishness, or a refusal to take him quite seriously?

A03 KEY CONTEXT

Ibsen's father, Knud, lost the family fortune through extravagance and reckless speculation. He became a heavy drinker, given to marital violence. Ibsen was to draw on his father's traits for many of his major characters. There is, perhaps, some hint of him in the offstage figure of Nora's father. Helmer is a definite contrast to him – and is very proud of his respectability.

Helmer's image of himself as the heroic protector finds an echo in much nineteenth-century literature that endorses the idea that men and women operated in different spheres. In his essay *Of Queens' Gardens*, Ruskin describes it in poetic terms that would appeal to Helmer the idealist: 'Man is eminently the doer, the creator, the discoverer, the defender ... But the woman's power ... is for sweet ordering ... she is protected from all danger and temptation. The man, in his rough work in the open world, must encounter all peril and trial.' (From *Sesame and Lilies*, 1865)

By the beginning of the twentieth century, some writers had begun to caricature Helmer's mix of anxiety, sexism and bad temper. One of the best-known caricatures is Mr Darling in James Barrie's *Peter Pan* (1904). He storms on stage crying to his wife, 'I warn you, Mary, that unless this tie is round my neck, we don't go out to dinner tonight, and if I don't go out to dinner tonight I will never go to the office again, and if I don't go to the office again you and I will starve, and our children will be thrown onto the streets.' (The Definitive Edition of the Plays of J. M. Barrie, Hodder and Stoughton, 1943, p. 507)

Study focus: A tragic flaw **A02**

Helmer's **tragedy** is that he does not know himself. He is successful as a barrister and a bank manager. Both these professions have very clear rules. He enforces these and avoids anything that could be described as not 'quite nice' (Act One, p. 30). This convinces him that he is a person of integrity, entitled to judge a man like Krogstad. In fact he is simply a conformist: it does not occur to him to question the rules. He is notably absent from the debate about moral health and the community in Act One (p. 39). Real concern for ethics might lead him to condemn Nora. Christian mercy (he feels that religion should shape her conduct) might understand that she acted from love. Instead he gives her no chance to explain herself. (**Ironically**, only Krogstad does this.)

Helmer appears to have bent the rules to help Nora's father (Act Two, p. 61) and has never been found out. When he thinks he is in the power of Krogstad as a result of Nora's forgery, Helmer's chief concern is how he will appear to others. Though his real preoccupation is with reputation, not morality, he seems blind to the distinction. When Nora mocks his refusal to reinstate Krogstad because he dislikes the way he addresses him by his Christian name, Helmer is comically – but genuinely – shocked. It does not occur to him that he is being 'petty' rather than exercising legitimate authority (Act Two, p. 63).

Masculine authority

In the same way he takes the rules of society for granted, Helmer also assumes that a title – such as 'husband' or 'employer' – endows him with a wisdom that cannot be questioned. He issues orders with absolute confidence in his expertise – about the use of Christian names, the eating of macaroons or how to dance the tarantella. He sees himself as a man of culture and education – an **idealist**. He feels competent to stage-manage Nora's dance and to lecture Mrs Linde about the aesthetic effects of a woman knitting or embroidering. This conviction of his own superiority persists through all the traumas of the final act. He is still confident that he can help Nora grow up, announcing, 'Playtime is over. Now the time has come for education' (Act Three, p. 98). He never realises that he is more interested in power than in the rights and wrongs of a situation. Nora is bitter about his refusal to pander to her 'moods and caprices' (Act One, p. 35) regarding the Italian holiday. He never actually admits that it was responsible for his present blooming health.

Heroic speech

Phrases such as 'Oh, don't be melodramatic' (Act Three, p. 94) suggest that Helmer imagines himself as a man of common sense and plain speaking. In reality, he is as self-dramatising as Nora. His stereotyped fantasy about rescuing her from 'terrible danger' (p. 92) comically disintegrates as he reads Krogstad's letter and cries, 'I am saved!' (p. 95). However, he bounces back to strike a new pose – the forgiving spouse. His **imagery** – 'I shall watch over you like a hunted dove which I have snatched unharmed from the claws of the falcon' (p. 96) – is comic, given that he has done nothing to rescue Nora from Krogstad. Instead of learning from his experience he convinces himself that he is the saviour in this situation. While by the end of Act Three Nora is able to look back more coolly on her expectation that he would take the blame on himself, Helmer produces another **cliché** of **melodrama**: 'no man can be expected to sacrifice his honour' (p. 102) – a phrase that fits the battlefield, not the bank.

The real doll in the house

Helmer is probably the least admirable character in the play. However he is not consciously selfish. As for many a nineteenth-century man, getting his own way seems synonymous with doing the right thing. While he preaches honesty and condemns Krogstad and untruthful mothers, he is blissfully unaware how sheltered his life is. The doctors hide his illness from him, his friend spares him a deathbed scene, his wife bustles Mrs Linde away so he will not have to see her sewing. Nora knows how to flatter him and he enjoys it, unaware of being manipulated. He thinks his decision to employ Mrs Linde is a result of her arriving 'at a lucky right moment' (Act One, p. 42). Nora would rather lie to him than challenge him, even over something as trivial as a bag of macaroons.

This might inspire our anger on his behalf, if his choices were considered ones. In fact, whenever Helmer acts for himself, it is on very confused moral grounds. Sometimes it is out of spite, like his dismissal of Krogstad; or from concern for his own reputation, as when he discovers Nora's crime. He is more pampered and indulged than Nora, a 'doll' protected from reality – by women out of deference to his masculinity, and by men out of concern for his weakness. However, it is difficult to take him too seriously. And it is rare for an audience not to feel some affection for a figure of fun. While Helmer has not outgrown his posturing and pomposity at the end of the play, it is worth noting that he no longer fusses about his own reputation but only about Nora's feelings for him. Perhaps he can change and make the 'miracle of miracles' (Act Three, p. 104) happen.

Key quotation: A typical response (A02)

Helmer's bewildered remark 'Nora, what kind of a way is this to talk?' (Act Three, p. 98) is his usual reaction to any suggestion of change – that is, to assume the speaker is making no sense at all (especially if the speaker is Nora).

(A03) KEY CONTEXT

Ibsen does not specify Helmer's age, but his first choice for the Swedish production of *A Doll's House* was the handsome young matinee idol Gustaf Fredricksen. He wanted him for his 'elegant and lovable light-heartedness' (Robert Ferguson, *Henrik Ibsen*, Richard Cohen Books, 1996, p. 243). If Helmer is played as a young man, the pomposity of some of his language will underline the play-acting side of his character and the naive nature that underpins it.

(A05) KEY INTERPRETATION

A review of Anthony Page's 1997 production at the Belasco Theatre in New York pointed out that Helmer is 'the toughest role in the piece'. Owen Teale was a young and handsome Helmer with a rigid, upright posture in a stuffy black suit, who slowly revealed both latent violence and extreme vulnerability as he realised that he was losing his wife.

Christine Linde

Who is Christine Linde?

- She is an old school friend of Nora's, seeking work at Helmer's bank.
- She was once in love with Krogstad, but left him for a rich man who could support her family. Now a penniless widow, she offers to share her life with Krogstad.
- She believes that Nora must tell Helmer the truth, and forces the situation by refusing to let Krogstad destroy the evidence of Nora's forgery.

First appearance

Mrs Linde is a quiet and polite woman who is qualified to work in a bank. She is clearly meant to be played as a contrast to the healthy and athletic Nora. Her life has left its mark. Nora finds her pale, thin and not at once recognisable as her old school friend. She is physically frail, telling Dr Rank that she has to take the stairs 'slowly' (Act One, p. 39) and is feeling the strain of overwork. She talks about bereavement and poverty. The audience may be shocked by the absence of grief for her husband, not explained for some time. But there is no indication that she experienced any inner conflict over her marriage of convenience. She seems not to want to talk about it. Initially, it seems Mrs Linde's function in the play is to be a **foil** to Nora, with her happy marriage and her beloved children. Her air of tired experience makes Nora seem empty-headed – although Nora would be a far livelier and more entertaining companion.

Bringing out the truth

If Mrs Linde is patronising when she makes remarks such as 'those bits of fancy-work of yours' (Act One, p. 33), she perhaps has a right to be. She has worked at many jobs, from teaching to shopkeeping. If the actress chooses, she may show some envy. Anyone in Mrs Linde's position might covet children and generous spending money – even if Nora has had to sacrifice her pocket-money at the moment. Helmer clearly finds her worthy but dull. She seems content for this to be the case; she is grateful for the job he offers and perhaps realises that a more overtly capable woman would unnerve him.

As she questions Nora about the loan, her curiosity seems to be simply that of a concerned friend. She is essentially fulfilling the function of a **confidante** in allowing vital information to emerge. Her kindness is apparent in her concern for 'the [morally] sick' (Act One, p. 40) in her debate with Dr Rank. However, she also has stern moral principles. She fears Nora's naïveté may lead her into a dangerous sexual situation over the loan, which she imagines is from Dr Rank. She is angry with Rank, more educated and worldly-wise, for taking advantage of Nora. Her determination to help is strong – she maintains that Krogstad 'must' persuade Helmer not to read his letter (Act Two, p. 75) – but she is equally intent on learning the whole truth of the situation and plays a part in helping it to emerge.

AO2

Study focus: A New Woman

Note the subversive side to the quiet Mrs Linde. She may be tired, she may resent having to ask people like Helmer for work as if it was a favour, but she has a true passion for work – it has been her 'only joy' (Act Three, p. 82). This gives her an independence and modernity that make her highly unusual. She is an image of the New Woman (see **Historical context**). Helmer, who hates the sight of a woman doing something useful like knitting, cannot imagine this kind of female. Mrs Linde is the first person to understand Nora's pleasure in being 'almost like' a man (Act One, p. 37). Perhaps this develops Nora's independence and gives her the courage to take the course of action she does.

We also learn in the last act that Mrs Linde has gone further than Nora on the road to self-determination. She has chosen the partner of her future life in Krogstad. She has been brave enough to travel especially to find him. She does not wait for him to find the courage to renew the relationship but proposes herself that they 'join hands' (Act Three, p. 82). She has no illusions about him. But she is also certain of her own ability to see the best in him and help him change his life. She wants to be a mother, and she will mother his children. Mrs Linde, in short, has made herself an individual who makes choices. She has, as she bitterly explains, used that ability before, when she first rejected Krogstad for a richer man to help her mother and brothers. She cannot say for certain whether it was the right choice. She admits, 'I've often asked myself that' (Act Three, p. 81).

Truth at all costs

Mrs Linde is not the passive victim she appears in Act One: she owns her experience and the self it has made her. It is this, perhaps, that makes her so determined that there should be 'full understanding' (Act Three, p. 84) between Nora and Helmer. She may want to shake them both out of an unhealthy dependency – Nora on her ability to perform 'tricks' and Helmer on the myth of Nora's helplessness. The actress has a choice in where to locate her **motivation** for telling Krogstad to leave his letter in the box: in envy, in excessive optimism, or in genuine benevolence. Invariably, she will demonstrate that the deceptively dull Mrs Linde is the play's truthteller, just as Nora is the bringer of light.

Key quotation: Female sacrifice

AO2

Mrs Linde tells Krogstad that, 'a woman who has sold herself once for the sake of others doesn't make the same mistake again' (Act Three, p. 83). She is well equipped to understand the way Nora has been treated by her father and its consequences.

AO1 PROGRESS BOOSTER

Plays of the nineteenth century rely heavily on secrets. It will be helpful to make notes on the characters of Mrs Linde, Krogstad and Dr Rank about the things they know about Nora that Helmer does not.

AO3 KEY CONTEXT

One of the first actresses to play Mrs Linde in England was the American actress Elizabeth Robins, who performed at a matinee in 1891. She went on to play several major Ibsen roles, including Hedda Gabler, and claimed to be politicised by them. She became a campaigner for woman's suffrage and in 1907 wrote a play, *Votes for Women*, which is still performed today. When she died in 1952 her epitaph in the *Guardian* described her as 'the last of that little phalanx which let Ibsen loose on the English stage … with shattering results.' (9 May 1952)

Krogstad

Who is Krogstad?

- He is an employee at Helmer's bank, later dismissed.
- He has a questionable past and acts as a moneylender. Nora owes him the price of Helmer's holiday.
- Desperate to keep his job, he is blackmailing Nora about a signature she forged.
- Reconciled to his former love Mrs Linde, he relents.

Study focus: A different kind of villain

Krogstad's name means 'crooked'. Initially he appears to be a stock villain. Many early Krogstads focused on his more frightening aspects, such as his unexpected and forceful entrances. But Krogstad is complex, both in himself, and in terms of the way he relates to the development of Nora. He is not a natural blackmailer. He resents the fact that he has had to stoop to blackmail at all. His demands are so modest they are almost comic. He wants an ordinary job, which he has already been doing quite well – his 'humble position' (Act One, p. 45) at the bank. He feels it is realistic to expect that Nora can make this happen. Helmer's refusal to think about the idea probably strikes the audience, as well as Nora, as 'petty' (Act Two, p. 62). Krogstad's later forceful insistence perhaps springs from a realisation that he has overestimated his employer.

KEY CONTEXT A03

Victorian England found it difficult to accept the motivation of a man like Krogstad. In *Breaking a Butterfly*, Henry Arthur Jones's 1884 play that draws very heavily on the plot of *A Doll's House*, the blackmailer has an extra grudge against the heroine's husband – he stole her love from him. He announces villainously, 'You took her from me! You made it impossible for me to have her! Very well! She shall be neither yours nor mine! She shall be the gaol's! This woman, who is your pride and joy – I will make her your shame and disgrace! I will ruin her utterly!' (Script now in the Victorian and Albert Theatre Collection.)

A mirror of Nora

Nora rejects the idea that Krogstad resembles her, because she cannot imagine his motive for forgery to be as unselfish as hers (Act One, p. 49). Although he gives no details, it is unlikely that Krogstad could have been as ignorant as Nora was of the risk he was running. But it is worth taking seriously his insistence on their similarity. Nora did *not* forge the signature to steal money, but to guarantee a loan which she has every intention of repaying. Such a crime hardly suggests a man infecting his family with 'the germs of evil' (p. 53). But, as he tells Nora, Krogstad has lost the appearance of respectability in a world run by men like Helmer.

By being treated as a criminal, Krogstad has been pushed into working at the edge of legality, where lies and petty harassment are rife. His agreement with Nora is legally binding, but he has carefully not asked questions about the name on the note, or about the fact that as a woman she has no right to sign the note. Bullying a client, as he does Nora, may be routine in his role as loan shark. He seems to be known for such work – Dr Rank knows and disapproves of Krogstad.

Progress booster: Fatherhood

A01

It is important to note that, although he despises Helmer, Krogstad is also driven by a powerful motive to become like him. Like Helmer, he is a father. His determination to 'fight for my little job at the bank as I would fight for my life' (Act One, p. 46) comes from a sense of responsibility to his children. As he tells Nora, 'My sons are growing up: for their sake, I must try to regain what respectability I can' (p. 46). Helmer may preach about Krogstad 'poisoning his own children with his lies and pretences' (p. 54). However, this is nothing to do with his real motives for dismissing him. As Krogstad bitterly remarks, neither Helmer nor Nora expresses any interest in his children. Note that Krogstad invariably refers to 'my children', while Helmer typically speaks of 'the children' or sometimes 'your [Nora's] children.' If you compare Krogstad to Helmer and the other two fathers we hear about, Nora's and Rank's, he is arguably the father who is presented the most positively in the play.

A blackmailer and his victim

While Krogstad hates his employer, he seems to have some respect for Nora. He carefully explains her criminal status without bitterness, to remedy her ignorance. The snobbish disdain with which she treats him does not really warrant this courtesy, but he does not lose patience with her. He is oddly compassionate in his warning against suicide: 'Most of us think of that at first' (Act Two, p. 72). He is quite brutal as she continues to fantasise about heroic sacrifice, but also practical, pointing out that he will still have the paper whether she dies or not. This is an apologetic kind of brutality, which never reaches the level of Helmer's rage against Nora in Act Three.

Second chances

Krogstad clearly loved Mrs Linde in the past and has continued to miss her. It takes time for him to accept that she still cares about him. He cannot fully trust her, but he also, perhaps, does not think of himself as lovable. He tells Mrs Linde that 'life has taught me to distrust fine words' (Act Three, p. 81), perhaps a reference to his treatment by Helmer. Once he is convinced that he is loved, he is decisive and immediately decides to return Nora's note. This of course means he will have no evidence of the loan. He is willing to reach out to the person he sees as his double – Nora – at some cost to himself. As this also benefits the man for whom he has such contempt, it shows an admirable lack of malice. The relationship between Krogstad and Mrs Linde is refreshingly free from illusions. They have seen the worst aspects of each other, and they have no romantic illusions about male strength or female weakness.

A05   KEY INTERPRETATION

The critic Toril Moi sees the scene between Krogstad and Mrs Linde as confirmation that 'the figure of the pure and self-sacrificing woman had become no more than a well-worn cliché ... Insofar as Mrs Linde and Krogstad are counterpoints to Nora and Helmer, it is not least because they refuse to build their marriage on theatrical clichés.' (*Henrik Ibsen and the Birth of Modernism*, OUP, 2006, p. 232)

Key quotation: Krogstad asserts his rights   A01

Krogstad's question to Nora, 'Didn't it occur to you that you were being dishonest towards me?' (Act One, p. 49) comes as a surprise. Nora's guests have been talking about responsibility towards 'society', but this is the first time someone from the wider world has confronted her directly. Ibsen's audience would not have expected such a searching question to come from the villain of the piece.

Dr Rank

Who is Dr Rank?

- He is a close family friend who often dines with Nora and Helmer.
- He is dying from a hereditary illness, and confides this to Nora alone.
- He is in love with Nora, and shortly before his death he thanks her for the light she has brought into his life.

Study focus: The role of *raisonneur* **A02**

Our first sight of Dr Rank suggests that his function is that of *raisonneur* – a detached observer, offering advice to the **protagonists** but not changing the course of the action. This was a role familiar in **well-made plays**, often given to a doctor. His dispute with Mrs Linde, complaining that in a society obsessed with caring for the morally sick The 'healthy ones just have to lump it' (Act One, p. 40) makes him seem both harsh and flippant. It is only in Act Two, when Nora mentions his illness, that we realise Rank is speaking of himself as a morally, but not physically, healthy man, cut off from life because of the moral sickness of his father. His disease is clearly on his mind all the time. Mrs Linde mentions his depression during the Christmas celebrations. Rank rarely articulates his feelings. He is probably aware that Helmer is no more capable of dealing with this than with the physical aspects of Rank's deathbed. Rank seems to bear no malice towards Helmer for his limitations as a friend.

The inner man

It is only to Nora that Rank explains the real depth of his bitterness and rage. She is the only one who shares his ability to play with language. At times they slip into private codes with the ease of professional comedians. When they swap bawdy innuendoes over the silk stockings, it is this sense of being a double act that is really giving them pleasure.

Humour allows Rank to discuss the forbidden subject of his illness, but also reflects his sense that 'Laughter's all the damned thing's fit for!' (Act Two, p. 65). He seems to get no comfort from religion or philosophy. However, he does value the sense of belonging. He voices a real need to keep his place in the Helmer household as long as possible. Nora determinedly adds a reminder that he is at home 'with us' (p. 67) rather than 'with me'. Rank's affection for Helmer is real – but it is also clear that he cherishes a fantasy of being Nora's husband. His devotion is rooted in more than desire, and we have no reason to suppose he is not perfectly sincere in his wish to 'lay down his life' for her (p. 68).

Key quotation: Rank's philosophy **A01**

Rank's remark to Helmer, 'Why shouldn't one make the most of this world? As much as one can, and for as long as one can' (Act Three, p. 89) sounds like simple hedonism. Nora, however, will perhaps perceive it as showing courage in the face of his imminent death.

The nurse (Anne-Marie)

Who is Anne-Marie?

- She looks after Nora's children, and Nora trusts her enough to leave them in her care.
- She was Nora's own nurse after the death of her mother.
- She had to leave her own child to do this.

An important role

Although small, the role of the nurse is important. We first see her surrounded by happy children. She is obviously good at her job. Nora's concern at how cold she is suggests that Anne-Marie cares more about the children's enjoyment than her own comfort. She may see herself as the real authority figure in the nursery. Nora asks to be allowed to take off the children's coats as a sort of treat, rather than assuming that she can do so. Anne-Marie preserves the boundaries between servant and mistress; although obviously worried when Nora begins to avoid the children, she asks no questions. There is real affection between the two women, however.

Making Nora

It is probably the nurse who is responsible for the fact that Nora feels most comfortable with people who are not authority figures, such as her father's servants or Dr Rank. The pride she feels in Nora's beauty as they get her costume ready for the party suggests that her motherly feelings are still very much alive. So does her response to Nora's peevishness about the state of her fancy dress – the nurse will not put up with seeing a perfectly good outfit thrown away. She tells her to have 'a little patience' (Act Two, p. 55). The actress playing the nurse might want to develop the **subtext** of this to suggest a concern for Nora's marriage.

Whether or not Anne-Marie is aware of the situation, it is clear that Nora trusts her old nurse to bring up her children. In the final act it will be important that we like and trust the character. Although the nurse does not appear, we will judge Nora on leaving her children less harshly if it is clear they are in good hands.

The hardest life of all

Of all the characters in *A Doll's House*, Anne-Marie has suffered most. She has known poverty and disgrace. Betrayed by 'that good-for-nothing' (Act Two, p. 56), she had no option but to give up her own child. Her suffering contrasts with that of the main characters – in the end, all their pain is about a piece of paper. Even Krogstad has managed to keep his children. The dignity and optimism with which Anne-Marie has made a new life and accepts its limitations is a silent comment on Nora and Helmer's future prospects. It is possible to change and live differently, but it is also undeniable that the world can be a harsh and unforgiving place.

A05 **KEY INTERPRETATION**

In *Ibsen: A Dissenting View* (CUP, 1977) Ronald Gray shows how Ibsen can still be misunderstood in exactly the same way as he was in the nineteenth century. He considers Nora's expectations 'unrealistic', but – just as in the 1870s – this is perceived as *Ibsen's* problem. The presence of the nurse is labelled a 'dramatic flaw': she is not a factor in Nora's choice to leave, but a convenience to prevent our 'full recognition of how bleak and unrealistic [Nora's] decision is'. For further critical views, see **Part Four**.

A03 **KEY CONTEXT**

The practice of wet-nursing (employing a woman to breastfeed a child not her own) is an old one and the figure of the nurse as **confidante** is common in literature of all periods. One of the most famous is the nurse in Shakespeare's *Romeo and Juliet* (c.1595), who plays a major part in the action. The figure of the nurse stands for affection and common sense. Anne-Marie's sad but realistic view of life and her care of Nora fit this image.

Key quotation: A mother figure   **A01**

The nurse comments to Nora that, 'you never had any mother but me' (Act Two, p. 56). It is an insight into her own kindness and Nora's loneliness. How might the audience respond to this image of motherhood?

THEMES

The individual and society

Progress booster: Defining a self

Think about the play's title in relation to Nora's statement, 'I am first and foremost a human being' (Act Three, p. 100). A doll is not a person; its character is determined by its owner. The owner chooses the functions it is expected to serve – baby or fashion model, for instance. Nor does a doll have a role in public life. Nora here is claiming the right to create her self rather than remaining in a 'doll's house'. Her argument is an **existential** one.

Existentialism is the idea that we are not born with innate characteristics but create ourselves through the choices we make. Hence it is important that individuals should have the freedom to choose their beliefs and actions. A self is shaped by using one's personal responsibility for choices. You can identify key choices made by Nora as the play progresses, and see the effect that those choices have on her character.

Taking Nora for granted

At the beginning Nora is defined by other people. For Helmer she is a pet, a sexual partner, a mother and a housekeeper. We see her adopt all these roles. She makes one choice – forging her father's signature – but this is on an impulse, rather than a considered decision. More importantly, it is secret. Nora imagines it can make no difference to who she is unless she is found out. (Before Krogstad hammers the point home, she never thinks of herself as a criminal.) Even work is a kind of play or disguise: 'like being a man' (Act One, p. 37). Her lack of interest in society – 'I think it's a bore' (Act One, p. 40) – means that she does not join the debate between Mrs Linde and Dr Rank about our responsibility to the world. For many nineteenth-century thinkers this was not a woman's problem. Defining a self was a male task, a 'struggle with the external world and with himself' (Toril Moi, *Henrik Ibsen and the Birth of Modernism: Art, Theater, Philosophy*, 2006, p. 245). 'Wife' or 'mother', on the other hand, expressed what a woman was born to be, rather than choices she might or might not make to define herself.

Moral implications

Act Two shows Nora's dawning awareness that choices have moral implications. She realises that, while Dr Rank could save her, taking his money would change their friendship. Instead of mutual affection, there would be an unequal balance of power. Nora behaves in a morally responsible way. This contrasts with Helmer, panicking at the sight of Krogstad's letter. He is not honest enough to make a moral choice. Instead, he decides to appease Krogstad. He rejects Nora while demanding she act the roles of wife and mother to make him look respectable. Once he is 'saved', he thinks he can grant her the real roles once more – indeed, he thinks they are Nora's 'most sacred duties' (Act Three, p. 100).

Masculine arguments

At the end of the play, Nora can no longer accept Helmer as spokesman for the powerful forces in society. She feels that he, and they, have let her down. As a lawyer, Helmer has let her remain ignorant of the law. When speaking of religion he is a hypocrite – he calls it 'your religion' (Act Three, p. 100), as if it is not something men need. She will no longer allow him to define the roles of wife or mother for her, but plans to learn for herself. Already beginning to shape an individual self beyond these labels, she will find her own moral code in 'society'. This means enlisting the help of Mrs Linde and even Krogstad; and she will go 'home' (p. 99) – not as a dependent daughter, for her parents are dead, but as a woman in a place where she is known and can work and learn.

Key quotation: Nora's choice **A01**

Leaving, Nora tells Helmer, 'I must stand on my own feet if I am to find out the truth about myself and about life' (Act Three, p. 99). This could be seen as her first existentialist act as she sets out to find out who she is.

Death, disease and heredity

A Darwinist view

'Well, I suppose I must take you as you are. It's in your blood. Yes, yes, yes, these things are hereditary, Nora' (Act One, pp. 26–7). Helmer is convinced that Nora's first request for money proves she has inherited her father's extravagance. By the end of the play he sees her as a hopeless case: 'No religion, no morals, no sense of duty!' (Act Three, p. 93). He never wavers from the conviction that criminal tendencies can be inherited, a view shared by some (though not all) early readers of Darwin (see **Historical Context**).

However, between Helmer's two statements we have learned that Nora is only pretending to be extravagant. The money she appears to be wasting is in fact paying off the debt. While her father may have been knowingly involved in fraud or corruption, her 'crime' is due to ignorance. She says, defiantly, that 'I wish I'd inherited more of papa's qualities' (Act One, p. 27). We do not know what his better qualities were. Helmer never names them and perhaps does not like to discuss the subject. For Helmer the power of 'inheritance' seems to deny the individual any possibility of change. This former barrister does not appear to believe you can choose whether or not to obey the law. Criminality is in the blood (or not).

Key quotation: Nora and inheritance **A01**

Nora explains Dr Rank's illness: 'His father was a frightful creature who kept mistresses and so on' (Act Two, p. 57). She does not go into the question of inherited morality. Does she disagree with Helmer on the subject?

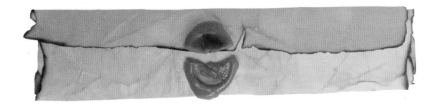

Physical inheritance or moral independence?

Dr Rank is surprisingly forgiving, referring to the father who passed on his disease as a 'gay young lieutenant' (Act Two, p. 65), rather than showing anger towards him. And the rage he does feel is not for himself alone. He resents the injustice of hereditary disease: 'And in every single family, in one way or another, the same merciless law of retribution is at work –' (Act Two, p. 65).

However, Rank's inheritance is biological, not moral. He seems to have chosen bachelorhood, so that his illness will die with him. He only tells Nora he loves her when he is near death. Indeed, he only uses the word in the past tense: 'That I have loved you as deeply as anyone else has? Was that horrid of me?' (Act Two, p. 68). Rank's integrity contradicts Helmer's theories about Nora's inherited morality. This never occurs to Helmer, even though he is Rank's best friend.

Moral sickness

Both Helmer and Rank use the **metaphor** of corrupt behaviour as moral sickness. For Helmer its source is the home, and the sickness invariably spreads. He lectures Nora about 'mothers who are constitutional liars', who infect their children with 'the germs of evil' (Act One, p. 53), reinforcing the work of heredity. Rank uses the expression differently: Krogstad is 'a moral cripple' (Act One, p. 39) – an individual damaged by his own actions, to whom society should behave with limited compassion. He argues with Mrs Linde's about society's responsibility to care for those 'sick' in this way (p. 40). Although the two never continue their discussion after this scene, Krogstad's change of heart, brought about by Mrs Linde's faith in him, suggests that she has won the argument.

Death

The play is full of graphic images of death. Rank imagines his own body 'rotting up there in the churchyard' (Act Two, p. 65). He knows how appalling the last stage of his illness will be. Nora also intends to die, in 'icy black water' (Act Three, p. 92). But she is not allowed to make this a romantic picture – Krogstad's mocking description of her corpse floating up bald and hideous in the thaw has already made that impossible (Act Two, p. 73).

Krogstad and Helmer, for all their differences, share the opinion that suicide is not a noble sacrifice, even if it is an admission of responsibility. The play moves the audience, too, towards that conclusion. Dr Rank's final resentment at leaving his life without even being able to offer 'the most wretched token of gratitude' (Act Two, p. 67) to change the life of someone he loves, reminds us that as long as people hold on to life, they can also change it for the better.

Revision task 6: The moral debate (A03)

The characters hold differing views on social responsibility. Write about:

- The views that Nora hears
- The conclusions she draws, explicitly or implicitly

Theatricality

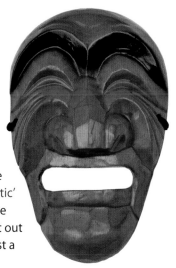

False manners

Ibsen often told his actors to avoid 'theatrical accents' and copy the life they saw around them, not other actors. He wanted his audience to respond to 'Nora' or 'Krogstad' rather than to someone they had already labelled '**ingénue**' or 'villain'. But Nora and Helmer themselves are influenced by the idea of performance. When Helmer says, 'Don't be melodramatic' (Act Three, p. 94), he thinks Nora is insincere about her possible suicide. But he is unaware that he too is playing a part straight out of the popular theatre – the 'man dishonoured', rather than just a husband whose wife has made a stupid mistake.

Acting in real life

It is when Nora and Helmer are consciously involved with performance that they reveal themselves most clearly. The fancy dress party offers a chance to 'stage' their lives to themselves and make sense of them. The subject of Nora's Capri dress and the dance she performs in it recurs throughout the play. Helmer's choice of this costume shows what he wishes Nora to be: a **symbol** of his sexual and social status in possessing a beautiful wife. Rank and Nora both grasp the significance of the silk stockings.

Helmer sees Nora's dance as an expression of his own talent. He is taking on the role of Pygmalion, the legendary sculptor who produced a statue so beautiful that he fell in love with it and it came to life. But Helmer forgets two things about the nature of performance. First, it requires dull backstage work as well as inspiration. Helmer is offended at the sight of women working, which includes Mrs Linde mending the Capri dress. Second, performance is a collaborative art. Nora and Rank shape the impromptu performance, not Helmer alone. Nora's tarantella is an outlet for the panic and terror she feels. She chooses to perform this dance about death in her own style – which Helmer condemns as 'a trifle too realistic' (Act Three, p. 85).

Understanding performance

Nora's 'tricks' (Act Three, p. 98) – the 'skylark' and 'squirrel' games, the pleading and persuasion – at first seem like harmless fun. She comes to realise that they hide the problems in her marriage from herself as well as Helmer, but struggles to find a new way to behave. Rank remarks to Nora that at the next party she should play 'the Spirit of Happiness' – by being herself (Act Three, p. 90). This is an expression of gratitude for what she has meant to him. But it is also a reminder that she is an individual as well as a wife. It is through exploring roles – wild dancer or noble suicide – that Nora stops acting out stereotypes and begins to discover who she is '*in her everyday dress*' (Act Three, p. 96).

Key quotation: Abandoning the part **A01**

As she is leaving, Nora tells Helmer, 'I don't accept things from strangers' (Act Three, p. 104). It is as if Helmer has no personal identity beyond the stereotype of manhood he performs. Perhaps all his character traits are formed by it?

A05 **KEY INTERPRETATION**

You can read about Ibsen's approach as a director of plays in Toril Moi's *Henrik Ibsen and the Birth of Modernism: Art, Theater, Philosophy*, OUP 2006

A03 **KEY CONTEXT**

Henry Arthur Jones's 1884 adaptation of *A Doll's House*, *Breaking a Butterfly*, contains the scene that exists in Nora's imagination when she thinks Helmer will behave like a hero from a **well-made play**:

DUNKLEY [THE VILLAIN] Tomorrow I will have her arrested on a charge of forgery!

HUMPHREY (*very calmly*) You make one mistake, Mr Dunkley! My wife did not forge that note.

DUNKLEY Not? Then who did?

HUMPHREY I did!

DUNKLEY You?!

HUMPHREY Yes – I! Now do your worst to me. You shall not touch a hair of her head!

Flora rushes forward with a shriek and falls at Humphrey's feet.

Curtain.

Money

A piece of paper and its meanings

Nora borrows £250 to do something useful. However, in the play the money never appears. It is represented by a piece of paper. This stands not just for a sum of money but for false promises and the misuse of power – a symbol of the Helmers' marriage. Nora's action has made her a criminal. It was illegal for a wife of the time to borrow money; her only source would be a dishonest lender. However, Nora's act has also brought her into a new world. When she says, defiantly, 'It was I who wrote pappa's name' (Act One, p. 49), she is admitting forgery – but also claiming her place in a man's world, in which men do not seem to behave with the honesty they expect from women.

Money and men

Helmer condemns Nora, but she is in this situation because he fears the power of money. Although his job at the bank involves borrowing and lending, he cannot cope with debt to save his own life. However, in accepting money from his father-in-law, a man he knew was involved in questionable dealings, Helmer has been a hypocrite. Nora remarks to Mrs Linde that 'Torvald likes to live well' (Act One, p. 36). That black Havana cigar in Act Three would not be cheap. While Helmer talks airily about sacrifices in Act One, Nora is the one who has had to make them. She struggles to do so honestly. This is not easy, because for those closest to her money is bound up with sexuality. Mrs Linde assumes the loan is from Dr Rank. Helmer is generous with the housekeeping but does not treat it as Nora's right. He enjoys being coaxed into giving it like a gift, never acknowledging that letting him 'live well' has a price.

Study focus: Money and productivity

Notice that nobody in the play produces anything of value. Helmer earns his money in a bank, controlling the flow of cash in the community. As a loan shark Krogstad does the same on a more dishonest level. The other characters (except Dr Rank) serve the bank: as clerks, like Mrs Linde, and Krogstad; as servants to the bank manager; or, in Nora's case, as his wife. Helmer no longer practises law, and Dr Rank is now unable to doctor anyone but himself. The 'society' debated in Act One is controlled by money, which dominates relationships throughout the play.

Key quotation: Nora and money

Nora tells Mrs Linde, 'In case you don't know, in the world of business there are things called quarterly instalments and interest' (Act One, p. 36). She takes pride in her familiarity with such things; it might surprise the audience to hear this kind of language from her.

Revision task 7: Wealth and debts

Consider the power relationships between characters. Write about:

- The power that money gives them (or not)
- What they owe to one another in non-monetary terms

PROGRESS CHECK

Section One: Check your understanding

These tasks will help you to evaluate your knowledge and skills level in this particular area.

1. What does Helmer have to say about Nora's early life? What does she say about it? Write your points in a two-column table.
2. What was the former relationship between Mrs Linde and Krogstad? Can they restore it? Make brief notes.
3. Nora says that she needs to educate herself. Make a list of the skills or ideas she might need or want to learn.
4. What does Helmer expect of a wife? How does this affect his behaviour as a husband? Write your ideas in a two-column table.
5. What economies does Nora make? Make a list and note whether they are successful.
6. Which characters come into contact with the paper containing the signature? Make a list, with short notes on how each character might feel about it.
7. Find three instances in which a character behaves melodramatically – like a figure in a play. Make notes on the effect this has on them and on the characters observing them.
8. What lies are told in the play, and why? Write your ideas in a two-column table.
9. Which character in the play do you think most closely resembles Nora in terms of their situation? Make brief notes explaining your reasons.
10. Helmer thinks that morality is inherited. Is there any justification for his view in the play? Make a list of points for and against the idea.

Section Two: Working towards the exam

Below are three tasks which require longer, more developed answers. In each case, read the question carefully, select the key areas you need to address, and plan an essay of six to seven points. Write a first draft, giving yourself an hour to do so. Make sure you include supporting evidence for each point, including quotations.

1. 'Nora is a selfish character throughout the whole play.' Do you agree?
2. Discuss the images of 'sickness' in the play. Does the play offer any definition of 'health'?
3. Consider the ways in which Ibsen uses disguise, theatricality and role-play in *A Doll's House*.

Progress check (rate your understanding on a level of 1 – low, to 5 – high)	1	2	3	4	5
The key actions, motives and thoughts of major and minor characters in the text					
The different ways you can interpret particular characters' words and actions					
How characterisation is linked to key themes and ideas					
The significance of key themes and ideas within the text					
The part played by learning and teaching in the different strands of the plot					
How some key themes (such as illness, death, dressing-up) are linked to context					

GENRE

Naturalism

One of the first people to see *A Doll's House* on stage, the critic Erik Bøgh was amazed to see a play 'so simple in its action and so everyday in its dress' (quoted in Meyer, *Ibsen*, Penguin, 1985, p. 477). He did not use the word **naturalism**, perhaps because not many of his readers would know it. But the play is an early example of this in its style and its aim. Naturalistic playwrights wanted to explore the people of their own time in their environment, just as sociologists or psychologists did. Consequently they abandoned a large number of theatrical conventions: actors addressing the audience, songs and dances not called for by the story, divine intervention or magical solutions.

Instead, they showed human behaviour and they also explained it by setting it in context. Nora is the product of a world that fails to educate women or recognise them as equal to men. Rank suffers not because he is being punished by God for his own sins, but as a result of his father's actions. Anne-Marie's life has been shaped by society's attitude to sex. Everybody is directly affected by the way money operates in their world. Naturalism needed a radically new approach to acting. Ibsen was fortunate in being able to work closely with his actors.

Political and social protest writing

Naturalism emerged during a period of social, political and intellectual upheaval. It is not surprising that some writers seized on the style to portray major social problems such as women's rights, sexually-transmitted disease and slum landlords – and implicitly demand change. The novelty of seeing a 'real' world rather than one of artificial backdrops and heightened language attracted audiences, even if the material could be uncomfortable. George Bernard Shaw, who saw Ibsen as a pioneer and model, noted that he made the audience into 'guilty creatures sitting at a play' (*The Quintessence of Ibsenism*, 1932 edition, p. 63).

Rather churlishly, Ibsen remarked after a dinner in his honour at the Norwegian Women's Union, 'I must decline the honour of deliberately having worked in the interests of the woman-question' (Ferguson, *Henrik Ibsen*, p. 416). But even if *A Doll's House* does not contain an outright plea for social change, it fulfils an important criterion for social protest writing. It shows the inequality of power and its results. It was impossible for feminism not to take inspiration from Nora. Women wrote their own dramas with Ibsen as model – for example, Elizabeth Robins in *Votes for Women* (1907). When naturalism became the dominant theatrical form, its social impact lessened. But it remained – as it was for Ibsen – a way to help society understand itself and to show people as responsible for their own lives.

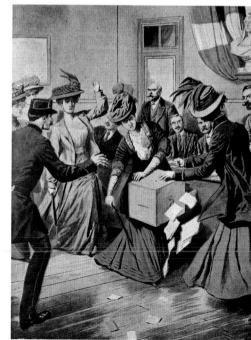

STRUCTURE

The well-made play

A Doll's House has a clear basic structure – that of the **well-made play**, as devised by the hugely popular French dramatist Eugène Scribe (1791–1861). First, the **exposition** sets up the situation. Nora's conversations in Act One with Helmer, Mrs Linde and Krogstad tell us all we need to know in order to understand how pressing the situation is. The curtain falls on a note of **suspense** with Krogstad's first demand. Act Two is taken up with the **development and complication** of the story. Nora struggles to find a way out, first by changing Helmer's mind, then by asking for Dr Rank's help. The action reaches a crisis when all her possible solutions fail. Nora's tarantella – a frantic attempt to postpone the reading of Krogstad's letter – makes a **strong curtain**.

Act Three drives towards the climax. Ibsen develops the suspense by hinting that a **resolution** is about to happen. Krogstad's change of heart could mean the letter will be destroyed. Then Ibsen closes that possibility with Mrs Linde deciding to reveal the truth. He builds up further suspense by making Dr Rank delay Helmer's reading of the letter. At last, he reaches what Scribe called the *scène à faire*: the confrontation between Nora and Helmer. This is the scene the audience has been eagerly expecting since the first act. At the **dénouement**, the revelation of all secrets, the original audience would expect something like Helmer's luxurious meditation on forgiveness. Shockingly, it only happens after his selfishness has rendered it meaningless. The real **resolution** – when the well-made play generally ties up all loose ends – also proves to be a reversal of expectation. Nora's quiet announcement that she is leaving her marriage is not so much an ending as the beginning of a new story.

Progress booster: Darkness to light

Note how, in addition to the 'well-made' model, the play has a clear individual structure. It takes place over three days. Reminders of the time increase the suspense. However, each act takes place at a different time of day. Days in a Norwegian winter are short and Christmas is near the shortest day. Nora's shopping trip will have made the most of the daylight – it is not long after sunrise. In Act Two Nora calls for the lamp during her conversation with Dr Rank. It is evidently mid-afternoon and growing darker. In Act Three we hear the party upstairs break up; it cannot be much earlier than midnight. The final conversation therefore takes place in the small hours of the next day. The overall sense is that Nora is living through a single day. Like her inner journey, it goes from light into profound darkness – with, perhaps, the hope of a return to the light. You may find that imagining the lighting at particular moments helps to understand the mood Ibsen is establishing.

Revision task 8: Alternative curtain lines

The structure of the play involves strong curtain lines and a powerful dénouement, all focused on Nora. Write brief notes to suggest how each act might end if the central figure was:

- Krogstad
- Mrs Linde

LANGUAGE AND DRAMATIC METHODS

Translation

It is worth bearing in mind that no English version of *A Doll's House* will give exactly the sense of Ibsen's *Et dukkehjem*. One translator may choose to be as accurate as possible. Another may prefer to replicate the impact of the original and find an English equivalent for a Norwegian expression. For instance, a Norwegian might address an official like Helmer by the professional title *Direktor*, as Mrs Linde does in Act Three (in the edition used in these Notes, Meyer has Mrs Linde calling Helmer 'Mr Helmer' – see p. 87).

Victorian England was fortunate to have the bilingual William Archer to provide a speakable translation. Earlier versions were, to say the least, bizarre: one by the Danish schoolteacher T. Weber became notorious – justly, as you can see below. But no translation can be exact. Even the simplest sentence in translation carries a slightly different weight of meaning from the original. While this need not spoil our enjoyment or understanding of a play, it can be interesting to see how different translations slightly change a meaning.

Exit lines

Here are some different translations of Nora's last line in Act Three:

- 'That cohabitation between you and me might become a matrimony. Good-bye.' (T. Weber, translated 1880)
- 'That communion between us shall be a marriage. Good-bye.' (William Archer, 1889)
- 'Where we could make a real marriage of our lives together. Goodbye!' (James McFarlane, 1961)
- 'That our life together could be a real marriage. Good-bye.' (Peter Watts, 1965)
- 'That life together between us two could become a marriage. Goodbye.' (Michael Meyer, 1965)

The English playwright Harley Granville-Barker (1877–1946) offered a prize to any drama student who could say Weber's line with a straight face. It is worth a glance at Weber to realise that translation involves a great deal more than looking up words in a dictionary. The religious and mystical overtones of Archer's 'communion' suggest that Nora has very high expectations of marriage. For the translators of the 1960s, when churchgoing had declined, 'communion' sounded too religious for a woman who had just stated her intentions to find her own path rather than rely on the Church. By using the plural 'our lives together', McFarlane implies that if Nora and Helmer resumed their marriage their lives would run side by side; even, perhaps, that they would both have careers. Meyer's 'life together between us two' is more elaborate than 'our life together'. It forces the actress to slow the pace of the speech. It may sound as if Nora is pondering how unlikely that is, while Watts's more concise Nora may still consider it a possibility.

None of these translations is wrong. Ibsen's original could carry all these shades of meaning and leave the performer to choose how to say them. But the process of choosing a translation can teach the reader a great deal about the play.

Language and craftsmanship

Spontaneity and **colloquial** ease are not easy to achieve in **naturalistic** dialogue. The audience has to be given information that the characters must already know. Ibsen manages this with great economy. For example, it is perfectly believable for Nora and Helmer to talk about the cost of things as she comes in after a shopping trip. But it is also a way to let the audience understand their social and financial position. The knowledge that their prosperity is recent, and that Helmer has only just secured his new job, helps us understand how vulnerable both of them will be later. Helmer will feel his new status threatened by Krogstad, and Nora's happiness at the end of her financial struggles will be short-lived.

Study focus: Subtext

A02

Ibsen was one of the first playwrights to realise the possibilities of **subtext**. This means the energies that pulse underneath the actual words spoken, the aspects of the play that come alive through the actors' performance of the text. Sometimes characters are conscious that they mean more than they say.

For example, when Nora and Dr Rank discuss the forbidden topic of syphilis in language about food, they are showing not only an awareness of the scandalous nature of the subject but also the closeness of their friendship. It is clear that this friendship partly depends on their enjoyment of being a witty double act. But if they are proud of their control of language – as in the way they flirt outrageously over the silk stockings – they can be taken by surprise by their own directness. Dr Rank's declaration of love is sudden and spontaneous, as if he cannot bear to hide behind clever speech any more.

Finally, in the last act, they say a loving farewell through their **allusions** to 'light' (Act Three, p. 90). The imaginative language keeps Helmer out of the conversation, but it is also a way of acknowledging their shared history over the last few days. Over the course of the action, the word 'light' has acquired a **symbolism** for them that is highly personal. As Nora offers to light the cigar she indicates that she is giving what she can, even though they cannot be lovers. When Rank thanks her for the light, he refers to all that she means to him. The dignity of this goodbye is a marked contrast to Act Two, where Nora is too preoccupied with her own problems to pay proper attention to Rank's news of his illness.

A03 **KEY CONTEXT**

In his review of the first production of A Doll's House in Copenhagen, the critic Edvard Brandes wrote perceptively about one aspect of the dialogue: 'The dialogue's distinctiveness and strength lie in the fact that the characters don't talk *with* each other, although they talk *together*, for each is always only thinking about him- or herself, they misunderstand each other, even when they believe they understand each other.' (*Abroad and at Home*, Copenhagen, 4 January 1880)

A02 **KEY CONTEXT**

The noted director Konstantin Stanislavsky (1863–1938), who evolved his theories of acting from working on Ibsen texts, offers a useful definition of subtext as something that 'flows uninterruptedly beneath the words of the text, giving them life and a basis for existing... It is the subtext that makes us say the words we do in a play.' (*Building a Character*, 1949, pp. 107–10)

Revision task 9: Nora speaks

A02

Make notes on how Nora's speech changes when speaking to:
- Helmer
- Krogstad
- Dr Rank
- Mrs Linde

Language and repression

Her awareness of the possibilities of language allows Nora to grow. On the other hand, Helmer's lack of imagination makes him take even the last goodbye of Nora and Rank at face value. He never looks below the surface of his own language. For instance, he repeatedly employs the endearments 'skylark' and 'squirrel'. It never strikes him that these are wild creatures and that Nora's home has become a cage.

The audience, however, realises that Helmer has built a prison of language, not just for Nora but for himself. In their final confrontation he is at a loss. Although he is clearly in pain and repeatedly asks Nora to compromise a little, he cannot speak of his own feelings. It is up to Nora to find the language to articulate the possibility of change. Nora's longing to swear (Act One, p. 41) is perhaps frivolous. But it also indicates the importance she places on freedom of speech. Helmer's refusal to discuss subjects of importance with her has constituted a kind of censorship.

Soliloquies

Scattered throughout the play are moments when the language seems to resemble that of the popular dramas that Ibsen despised. Nora has a number of **soliloquies**, ranging from casual remarks such as 'Yes, he's here' (Act One, p. 24) to a speech at the end of Act Two that would not seem out of place in a **melodrama** or one of Scribe's 'candy-floss' plays (**see page 16**): 'Seven hours till midnight. Then another twenty-four hours till midnight tomorrow. And then the tarantella will be finished. Twenty-four and seven? Thirty-one hours to live' (p. 79).

Ibsen prided himself on getting rid of soliloquies in his previous play *The League of Youth* (1869) because he thought they were a clumsy way of giving the audience information. However, in *A Doll's House* he found a new use for them. Soliloquies like this one are not, in plot terms, strictly necessary. Their job is to tell us something about Nora's imagination. She is behaving as if she is living in a world of **well-made plays** where men make noble sacrifices for women and women make even nobler ones for men. By speaking to herself in this heightened language she is, in effect, trying on such a role.

Like Nora, Ibsen's original audience may have struggled to articulate new ideas about gender when their imagination and expectations were nevertheless shaped by these theatrical stereotypes. When Nora sits down and engages in a rational dialogue at the table, giving Helmer a carefully argued and logical analysis of what is wrong with her life, she shows that her understanding of the world has changed. She no longer expects a 'miracle' or a happy ending as if she lived in a world scripted by Scribe. Ibsen is challenging his audience to abandon such simplistic expectations of a play, or of men and women.

Staging

A room on stage

Ibsen's advice to writers was 'Use your eyes' (quoted in Michael Meyer, *Ibsen*, 1985, p. 501). The visual dimension of his play is as important as the dialogue. Most nineteenth-century theatres had a **proscenium arch** stage, a box like a room with the **fourth wall** missing,

but the actors interacted with the audience, speaking some of their lines directly to them. Instead, Ibsen wanted to give the sense that the characters had no idea that the wall was there – the audience was invisible to them. He reinforces the sense of 'real life' by using everyday objects with significant dramatic tasks. The Christmas tree, for instance, charts the passage of time and also reflects Nora's feelings. At first it shows her excitement about the festivities and the joy that the loan is soon to be paid off. As she decorates it, the gaudy ornaments embody her mixed feelings about 'dressing up' and pretending to be the kind of wife Helmer wants. Finally, its candles burnt out, it reflects her despair.

Study focus: Dramatic space **A02**

Note how space is used to illustrate Nora's journey to independence. The action takes place only in the living room, but there is a way out into the hall and two entrances to Helmer's study. Nora never enters through either of Helmer's doors. While others come and go freely in the hall, she seems increasingly shut in. We see her confidently entering the hall just once, at the rise of the curtain. Later she almost isolates herself in the room, sending the children away. Later still she is locked in by Helmer. Her final exit through the house is a slow reclamation of freedom. We hear her go through the spaces she has not been able to cross alone. We wait, with Helmer, to hear the final bang of the door to the outside world.

Costume

Costume is carefully chosen. There are men with money, Rank and Helmer, and their clothes are of good quality. They do not have to go out in the worst of the weather, and can put style before comfort. In contrast the employees, Krogstad and Mrs Linde, wear clothing that shows the relative harshness of their lives. Krogstad's bulky coat and furs give him a menacing appearance, though they are perfectly suited to the weather. Nora's stylish but cheap dress shows her secret economies. Her Capri outfit, on the other hand, reflects Helmer's fantasy of her as a child he can dress like a doll. Nora's relationship with this dress is complicated; note that she is reluctant to put it on to perform for Rank and Helmer. Throughout, too, we have seen Nora's outdoor clothing in the room, but she is not able to put it on and make a decision. Her final entrance in street clothes shows how firm her decision to leave is.

KEY CONTEXT

By the time he had written *The Wild Duck* in 1885, Ibsen felt confident enough in his lighting skills to write to the manager of the Kristiania Theatre, 'The lighting … is important; it is different for each act, and is calculated to establish the particular atmosphere of each act.' *A Doll's House* requires a similar attention to light and its role in shaping mood. Electric lighting opened up possibilities for emphasising the passage of time and change of atmosphere.

Lighting

Ibsen was writing during the transition from gas to electric light on the stage. It was not until writing *Ghosts*, two years after *A Doll's House*, that he could take the more subtle effects of electric light for granted. However, *A Doll's House* shows him using changes in lighting to underpin the mood of a scene. Nora's call for a lamp during her intimate conversation with Dr Rank in Act Two radically alters its tone – as Nora herself is aware.

As the curtain rises on Act Three, much of the available light is concentrated around the table; Mrs Linde has lit a lamp while preparing to talk to Krogstad. This will later be the setting for the final talk between Nora and Helmer. The light acts as a magnet to draw them together into the most intense exchange of their lives.

Music and dance

A **naturalistic** play is unlike other theatrical forms. It does not have the opportunity to use song and dance to intensify the action or provide entertainment – unless these form a part of the story itself. Nora's tarantella is carefully placed in the plot to provide a reason for this heightened form of expression. It creates immediate suspense – she is trying to postpone the end of her marriage and perhaps of her life. But it also gives us further insights into how Helmer persistently ignores her point of view; and into her complex relationship with Rank, who plays to match the wildness of her dance, as if encouraging her to express her feelings.

KEY INTERPRETATION

In David Thacker's production for television in 1992, Juliet Stevenson and Trevor Eve stressed the pain of the final break-up for Helmer. While Stevenson's Nora did not waver in her determination to leave, she tried her utmost to comfort Helmer, who wept like a child. She repeatedly sat down next to him, took his hand, and explained her decision very quietly rather than with anger.

Study focus: Comedy

One reason the ending of *A Doll's House* is so powerful is that, even if we approve of Nora's action, the grief she and Helmer experience is painful. The audience has an emotional investment in the sadness of this ending. An important part of Ibsen's technique to make us accept the reality of these characters is the use of comedy. Laughing and being moved by them makes our relationship with them more complex, more like the relationships we have in real life.

Ibsen uses a broad range of comic skills. There is a good deal of physical comedy, from Nora's little animal impressions to Helmer's drunken demonstration of how to look dainty while sewing. Some of the early exchanges between Nora and Helmer about money and macaroons are light-hearted, suggesting that the marriage has its happy moments with domestic in-jokes. Her risqué conversations with Dr Rank are a more sophisticated kind of wit. In both cases, though, the effect is of a bond maintained by shared fun. Laughter energises the play throughout and makes it clear to us that, although much is gained, real relationships are broken as Nora leaves.

PROGRESS CHECK

Section One: Check your understanding

These tasks will help you to evaluate your knowledge and skills level in this particular area.

1. Ibsen gives a number of stage directions to indicate that characters are doing something while they speak. List three of these and say what the action adds to our understanding.

2. Find three examples of women's financial dependency on men in the play. Make brief notes on how it affects them.

3. Find a conversation or speech which acts as exposition for the audience. Do you find it convincing as natural dialogue? Make brief notes.

4. Find three examples of a character communicating through subtext. Make brief notes to explain the feelings or ideas beneath the words.

5. Find an episode in which Nora tries and fails to express what she thinks to another person. What do you think is the problem in this case? Make brief notes.

6. Make short notes on Nora's first entrance in each act. What do we learn about her state of mind from each?

7. List the appearances made by the maid and make short notes on each to say what they add to our understanding of the Helmer household.

8. Make a list of the costumes worn by the men and write brief notes to say how they show their status and their character.

9. Ibsen makes use of a lighted lamp at several points. Make brief notes explaining what this brings to the stage picture.

10. Choose three comic moments and write brief notes on their dramatic effect.

Section Two: Working towards the exam

Choose one of the following three tasks which require longer, more developed answers:

1. The plays tells the story of one family's Christmas. Explore the relationship between the festivities and the action of the play.

2. The set (as described in the stage directions) has a number of carefully arranged doors. Choose three entrances or exits you think are particularly interesting and explain what they contribute to the play.

3. Find three instances where Nora is unable to say what she wants, and suggest the reasons for this.

A01 **PROGRESS BOOSTER**

For each Section Two task, read the question carefully, select the key areas you need to address, and plan an essay of six to seven points. Write a first draft, giving yourself an hour to do so. Make sure you include supporting evidence for each point, including quotations.

Progress check (rate your understanding on a level of 1 – low, to 5 – high)	1	2	3	4	5
How Ibsen structures the play					
How dialogue contributes to characterisation					
How an individual text can modify our understanding of a genre					
The dramatic effect of costume and costume changes					
The use of key images (sickness, light) and their effect on how we understand the relationships in the play					

Henrik Ibsen.

CONTEXTS

Historical context

New Norway, new language

Ibsen was born into a time of change. As the Napoleonic Wars ended, the Danish king ceded Norway to Karl XIV of Sweden. Norwegians had their own parliament but throughout Ibsen's life the struggle to keep their independence continued. There was growing enthusiasm for a specifically Norwegian culture, and for the newly-available written form of the Norwegian language, *landsmaal*. Danish was still the language of the cultured. No classical plays had been translated into *landsmaal*. The chance to write *landsmaal* gave Norwegian writers a real voice. To understand the limitations the old written forms had placed on them, it may help to imagine Ibsen's contemporary Emily Brontë trying to write *Wuthering Heights,* or Tony Harrison today trying to write *V*, without the language and rhythms of Yorkshire.

Industrialisation

At the time of Ibsen's birth in 1828, ninety per cent of the population of one million were involved in agriculture. Their way of life was not very different from that of the Middle Ages. By the time he was writing *A Doll's House*, the economy was capitalist and industrialised. Towns were linked by railways – Nora's travel plans are realistic – and the population had doubled in size. There were new social groups: an industrial working class, largely powerless; an expanding middle class, including clerks like Mrs Linde; and a more socially mobile bourgeoisie of lawyers and officials. Helmer is part of this latter group. Krogstad wishes to be.

Revolution

The year 1848 was one of revolutions in Europe. A radical reform movement in Norway led by Marcus Thrane defended the rights of poor farmers and factory workers. This was brutally put down with the aid of the Swedish monarchy, and the population was bitterly divided over the issue. Ibsen sympathised with the Thranists, but lacked the courage for direct action. Narrow Norwegian nationalism increasingly exasperated him.

In February 1864 Prussia invaded Schleswig. Karl XV of Sweden and Norway offered Denmark his support, only to find that the Norwegian parliament forbade it. By April the Prussian army had stormed the Danish town of Dybbol. Ibsen saw Danish cannon paraded in triumph through Berlin. He never forgave his country for the betrayal of its fellow Scandinavians. By 1882 the Norwegian left had won a significant election victory, but did little with its power. No party showed much interest in social change. The process of extending the vote was slow.

All these factors combined to make Ibsen cynical about politics. The central character in *An Enemy of the People* (1882), his play about bureaucracy and corruption in a small town, cries, 'The majority is never right.' Town officials ignore the state of the public baths, and as a result people die. In *A Doll's House,* the consequences are personal rather than social, but in Helmer, Krogstad and Nora's father we see some degree of corruption.

KEY CONTEXT **A03**

Landsmaal (known as *nynorsk* since 1929) was adopted as an official language in Norway in 1885. Before the advent of *landsmaal* the formal language used for writing was *riksmaal*, based on the Danish language.

KEY CONTEXT **A03**

Thirty-five years before Nora slammed the front door, Karl Marx made it clear that a political revolution which did not include giving women equal rights was inadequate: 'The most direct, natural and necessary relation of person to person is the relation of man to woman ... from this relationship one can therefore judge man's whole level of development' (*Economic and Philosophical Manuscripts*, 1844).

Study focus: New sciences

If Ibsen had been born into a rich family, he might have been one of the first people to have a photograph of themselves as a baby – the earliest photographs were produced the previous year. Photography continued to develop throughout Ibsen's lifetime, and fascinated him. It meant ordinary people like Nora and Helmer could record and interpret portraits of one another, a right once restricted to those rich enough to commission paintings.

New academic sciences which touched on ordinary lives had begun to establish themselves. Ibsen's son Sigurd was a pioneer of sociology, carrying out surveys and demographic studies of the Norwegian people. Suddenly the middle class was interested in itself. It was only logical that the theatre should show characters like Nora and Helmer – and that they should be shown discussing 'society'. Psychiatry was in its infancy; Sigmund Freud was born twenty-eight years after Ibsen and began research into mental disorders in 1885. It is no surprise that he was an admirer of Ibsen. Freud's concern with the way that everyday language can reveal **motivation** – through jokes, dreams, the choice of **metaphors** and slips of the tongue – made sense in a world learning to explore the **subtext** of plays.

Darwin

This was also the world of Charles Darwin. In 1859 he published *On the Origin of Species by Means of Natural Selection*. Rooted in close observation of the natural world, the book suggested that some species – including the human race – had survived by adapting themselves to existing conditions. It also claimed that other species vanished because they were less 'fit' to adapt. This undermined the literal interpretation of the Bible account of the Creation. For those who, like Ibsen, already struggled with the religious certainties they were brought up with, it meant that society had to devise moral codes for itself. *A Doll's House* (1879) and *Ghosts* (1881) were written just as new Danish translations of Darwin were being published.

Both plays explore questions of disease and heredity. Both show the struggle of an individual towards meaning in a life without religion. For Émile Zola, the pioneer of **naturalism** in fiction and the novel, this was as it should be. He felt that naturalism was the proper response to the blossoming of new sciences which were 'still very young, but they are growing and leading us to truth in a movement that is sometimes disturbing because of its rapidity. It is enough to mention cosmology and geology, which have struck such a terrible blow at the fables of religion' ('Naturalism in the Theatre', in *Documents of Modern Literary Realism*, edited by George J. Becker, 1963, p. 200). Nora's determination to think for herself rather than accept what the Church has taught her, and Helmer's shock at the very idea, would have found echoes all over Scandinavia.

Charles Darwin.

A03 KEY CONTEXT

In *Peer Gynt*, Ibsen uses the photographer Daguerre's technique of printing using silver salts as a metaphor for the making of a better self: 'I develop it. / I steam it and dip it, I burn it and cleanse it / With sulphur and similar ingredients, / Till the picture appears which the plate was intended to give. / I mean, the one known as the positive.' (*Plays: Six*, translated by Michael Meyer, p. 175.) Nora's stripping of false selves arguably reveals the image of the strong woman she has always been.

A03 KEY CONTEXT

Ibsen had been reared by his devoutly religious mother, Marichen, who was associated for some time with a sect called the Lammers. Although he discarded their beliefs, one habit of the Lammers was very relevant to theatrical naturalism. They forbade curtains, saying that people should allow their lives to be seen by everyone, just as Ibsen's theatre removed an imaginary 'fourth wall' to show images of real life.

Progress booster: The New Woman

It is worth noting points in the text which show how the world was changing for women. Industrialisation had opened up opportunities. As a boy Ibsen would have known many peasant women largely unaware of the larger world – perhaps like the young Anne-Marie. By the time he reached middle age, white-collar women like Mrs Linde were common. Norwegian women entered education in 1876, when the first girls sat the secondary school examination. By 1882 those who could afford it might go to university.

However, women workers – factory hands, teachers or office workers – earned less than men, had little prestige and, in the case of the middle class, had to give up work if they married. Across Europe, a middle-class man's social status was enhanced by a wife who remained at home. Although Helmer treats his 'skylark's' extravagance as a problem, he would be shocked to know that she could earn money. Like most men of his time he believes in separate spheres – the idea that the sexes were spiritually and biologically different; males were designed for the cut and thrust of work and women for childcare. You could see the play as the story of the making of a 'New Woman', as the nineteenth century labelled women like Nora who rejected their 'sphere'.

Political rights

Throughout Europe agitation for the rights of women was linked to the social changes taking place. Women who shared Nora's experience were speaking out. Flora Tristan (1803–44), for example, who campaigned for the rights of the working class in France, divorced her abusive husband and lost custody of her children. Mary Wollstonecraft published *A Vindication of the Rights of Woman* in 1792 – just three years after the start of the French Revolution. She gave a precise analysis of the real harm that underlay the belief in 'separate spheres' held by men like Helmer. She stated that women were educated to be 'pleasing at the expense of every solid virtue' (quoted in Joan Templeton, *Ibsen's Women*, 2001, p. 120) – rather as Nora has been taught to dance and to catch a husband but not to think for herself.

Nora as a model

Nora is perhaps the first female dramatic character of her time to be fully aware that she is at odds with her society. It is not surprising that the play found eager audiences and conservative critics all over Europe and America. 'The Woman Question', as it was called, embraced a great many issues. Anxiety about gender roles was acute. During Ibsen's lifetime the British Parliament passed new legislation about divorce, the age of consent, venereal disease and homosexuality. The women's suffrage movement in the UK was concerned with many aspects of women's lives besides the question of the vote. Their motto – 'Let justice be done though the heavens fall' – reflects Nora's rejection of the authority of the Law and the Church. Controversy over the play provided a natural focus for their activity.

Settings

A national theatre

Although the action of the play could take place anywhere in Europe, it was important to Ibsen to set *A Doll's House* in Norway. As soon as he began to study the theatre in Norway he complained, 'we produce nothing ourselves, neither do the Danes.' He understood that to produce new work would involve finding new forms. 'The truly nationalist writer', he explained, 'is one who understands how to provide his work with that basic keynote that sounds to us … from within ourselves.' (Robert Ferguson, *Henrik Ibsen*, Richard Cohen Books, London, 1996, p. 39) By 1857 he was artistic director to the Norwegian Theatre in Kristiania – and under pressure to produce some distinctively national drama. He did extensive research into Norwegian folk songs and stories, an especially notable result being *Peer Gynt*, published in 1867. Later, he shifted into a more naturalistic style, although his final works return to the mythic.

Real Norwegians

The Helmer household would be instantly recognisable as belonging to Norway's new middle class. The layout indicates that they have an apartment, rather than a house, suggesting modest prosperity rather than luxury. The pictures and items like the Capri dress show that they see themselves as part of a wider world, picking up souvenirs from their travels and enjoying European culture. But the stove, a typically Norwegian item of furniture, and Nora's tendency to drift to it for warmth, set the play firmly in Scandinavia.

The talk of Christmas in the text, and the use of light and costumes, locate the play in time too – this is the deepest winter, when night draws in soon after noon. The moving conversation between Nora and Dr Rank takes place in the growing darkness of the afternoon. Her final parting from Helmer takes place in the early hours of the morning, long before sunrise, stressing her need to be gone rather than wait for day. Nora's situation prompted women across Europe to change their lives. However, the **imagery** she dwells on when contemplating suicide – the dark and icy waters giving up their dead in the spring thaw (Act Two, p. 73) – situates the play very precisely in a Norwegian landscape of fjords.

Study focus: The house as a trap

Note that the play would have had at least one, probably two, intervals. Ibsen could easily have taken advantage of this to change the set and shift the location – to the study, or Nora's room, or even Krogstad's house. However, he chose to confine the action, and thus Nora herself, to a single room. It is the other characters, like Mrs Linde, who give us an indication of a country beyond where life is changing, especially for women. This is a Norway where people are moving into the cities and a woman can travel alone by boat or train in search of a better life. When you hear Nora finally slam the door, it is after a prolonged walk through the house. It gives us – and Helmer – the chance to reflect on her determination to follow through her declaration of independence. She finally has access to the new Norway.

Literary and theatrical context

General influences

Ibsen was fond of saying that he did not read books. This was not true – he read all of Dickens as a young man, and he admired the Russian novelists Dostoyevsky and Tolstoy for their realism and detailed observation. His intention, perhaps, was to remind the critics and journalists that, unlike most of them, he had not had an expensive education. However, he was a  passionate reader of newspapers and liked to converse with his friends and his wife Suzannah about current literary trends across the world. It was these sources, rather than literary works, that inspired the topicality of his ideas on issues like the rights of women and sexually-transmitted disease – what his friend Brandes called 'the low rumble that tells of ideas undermining the ground' (quoted in Meyer, *Ibsen*, 1985, p. 500). It is not easy to identify specific works that influenced him because he was such an original writer.

Rejecting idealism

Ibsen was clear about the kind of play he did *not* want to write. In the late eighteenth century, drama, like all the arts, was shaped by **idealism** – the idea that art should lead people to perfection by offering a vision of truth and beauty. While this had given rise to powerful and moving work, idealism had become stale. One of the key words of the older theatre was 'sentimental'. This originally meant 'giving rise to noble feelings'. By Ibsen's time it had come to mean 'full of cheap emotion' – the kind Nora learns to reject in favour of clear thinking. Idealist drama over-simplified characterisation, filling the stage with stereotypes rather than real people living in a recognisable environment affecting their daily life. Women in particular tended to be shown as saints or devils rather than complex characters. Ibsen wanted a drama that left the audience to draw their own conclusions, rather than tie up the ends of the story neatly. As he said, 'the true end lies beyond … it is now up to each one of us to find his or her own way' (quoted in Meyer, *Ibsen*, 1985, p. 162). However, the lack of good translations meant that he could not find European playwrights to use as models.

A structural model

Eugène Scribe (1791–1861; see portrait, left) was a prolific and popular dramatist. He wrote hundreds of plays designed to appeal to the middle classes, using a very specific formula which came to be known as the **well-made play**. It comprised an **exposition**, setting up a situation, a **development and complication**, involving many twists and turns in the plot, leading to an exciting crisis and a **dénouement** with sensational revelations. Ibsen, who directed a great many of Scribe's plays in Kristiania, despised Scribe's sensational stories and cheap emotion. However, the discipline of Scribe's structure had offered a way to contain the disorganised passions of idealist drama. It provided Ibsen with a framework in which to tell the stories he wanted.

Theatrical influences

Ibsen probably learned less from literary sources than from theatre practitioners. His work as a director had taught him how actors worked and how the theatrical space created or limited the possibilities for a play. But the most powerful influence on him was that of Duke Georg II of Saxe-Meiningen (1896–1914), a Prussian aristocrat whose theatre company touched Ibsen's imagination profoundly. The company had no stars. Even the actors playing the smallest roles were given a distinctive character to portray, just as Ibsen would characterise the servants in *A Doll's House*. Instead of the flapping backcloths lit by flickering chandeliers that Ibsen resented in the Norwegian theatre, Saxe-Meiningen used materials such as metal and stone. The solidity of his sets inspired the realistic-looking domestic interior of the Helmer household. Once Ibsen was aware of a company with both the vision and the acting skills suited to a naturalistic style, he advanced with greater confidence. His first play to explore stage naturalism fully was *The Pillars of Society* in 1877.

Ibsen as an influence

The flourishing of **naturalistic** drama at the end of the nineteenth century was partly due to Ibsen himself. The most developed performance techniques of naturalism emerged from the Moscow Art Theatre, founded by Vladimir Nemirovich-Danchenko (1858–1943) and Konstantin Stanislavsky (1863–1938) in 1898. Ibsen had provided Stanislavsky himself with a successful acting role, Dr Stockmann in *An Enemy of the People*. It was through reflections on this performance that Stanislavsky began to evolve the 'system' by which naturalistic actors have been taught ever since, learning to achieve an intense focus on their characters' desires and shutting out awareness of the audience beyond the **fourth wall**. In Britain, opportunities to see Ibsen in the theatre were limited by the censor, but in private clubs and readings radicals like George Bernard Shaw and Harley Granville Barker (1877–1946) dealt with social issues. Granville Barker took over the Royal Court Theatre in 1904, developed an acting style that freed English actors from staginess and equipped them to work with Ibsen and his successors.

Ibsen's legacy

Theatre practitioners today work in a variety of styles, and naturalism is just one option. However, writers with a strong social message often work in the tradition established by Ibsen. Arthur Miller (1915–2005) explicitly acknowledged him as a model. Miller's play *All My Sons* (1947) closely resembles the plays of Ibsen, with a solidly-constructed story about a pillar of society who has a guilty secret (see photo of the 2010 production, above). An emerging new form, verbatim theatre, has examined social issues as diverse as prostitution and the London riots. Alecky Blythe's plays *The Girlfriend Experience* (2009) and *Little Revolution* (2014), for example, use the actual words of people talking about their daily lives and how these issues affect them. The author selects and structures a mass of recorded material into a precise structure. The lines are carefully repeated by actors to replicate the exact inflections of the original speaker.

Ibsen would often develop the story of a minor character in his next play. If you read several of his plays in sequence, it is like looking at different sections of one large community. His friend Brandes admired a character in Ibsen's 1869 comedy *The League of Youth*, who complains: 'You dressed me up like a doll. You played with me the way one plays with a child' (Act 3). He suggested she deserved a play to herself. While acting on the suggestion with *A Doll's House*, Ibsen decided to develop the story of Dr Rank. The central character of his next play, *Ghosts*, has a similar inherited disease.

Arthur Miller translated Ibsen's *An Enemy of the People* (his version was staged in 1950) and wrote in his preface to the published edition: 'There is one quality in Ibsen that no serious writer can afford to overlook. ... It is his insistence, his utter conviction, that he is going to say what he has to say, and that the audience, by God, is going to listen. ... Every Ibsen play begins with the unwritten words: "Now listen here!"' Do you find this quality in *A Doll's House?*

KEY CONNECTION A04

The narrator of Khaled Hosseini's novel *The Kite Runner* tells how his gift for words led him to become a writer. While he does not struggle with articulacy, he betrays his half-brother by not speaking out when he is attacked, and his young nephew by making rash promises. When to speak, and to whom, is key to Nora's development too: only at the end of the play can she explain herself clearly to Helmer.

Comparative texts

Social protest: speaking out

Social protest writing often explores the journey of an oppressed or marginalised person towards articulacy. Nora initially uses childlike expressions like 'heaps and heaps of money' (Act One, p. 30) and 'Pooh' (Act One, p. 34), in contrast to those around her. Later, she utters balanced, logical sentences, even when talking about her own ignorance: 'I've learned now that certain laws are different from what I'd imagined them to be; but I can't accept that such laws can be right.' (Act Three, pp. 100–1). It is a vivid study of empowerment.

Tony Harrison's poem *V* also concerns the voice of the powerless. It is a dialogue between the poet and an unemployed football fan spraying obscenities in a graveyard. The sprayer's analysis of his motivation is sharp, shaming anyone who might dismiss him as a vandal. But he is not interested in having the poet speak for him nor, seemingly, to be involved in political action. He is less an individual in his own right than an aspect of the poet himself. *V* firmly asserts the value of both poetry and the sprayer's angry energy. But while Nora walks into a world that is beginning to change, *V* expresses a hope for understanding in a society that will not change.

Poetry, drama and stereotype

Narratives in all media draw on pre-existing stories and character types; these often help to make their original material more vivid and comprehensible. Both Chaucer's *Merchant's Tale* and *A Doll's House* make use of stereotyped characters and situations, although they are used differently. Ibsen shows a woman abandoning **melodramatic** stereotypes on a journey to self-discovery. She achieves it through interactions with other rounded characters. The play would be dull if they were less complex.

KEY CONNECTION A04

Blake's poem 'The Garden of Love' in *Songs of Experience* is a vivid image of the damage done by the rigid enforcement of rules and doctrines. Nora's journey through the play could well be seen as a transition from innocence to experience. Like the speaker in the poem, she sees the Church as 'binding' her into an impossible situation and crushing her natural desire to make her own choices.

Chaucer's tale, however, reveals one individual by showing a cast of characters through his eyes. The Merchant, who seems to have bitter marital experience – 'Of myn owene soore, For soory herte, I telle may namoore' (II, 1243–4) – chooses an old tale expressing a stereotyped view of young wives as disloyal and deceptive. He develops it to assert the truth of that stereotype. His protagonist is not merely an old fool, he is an old fool who marries in the teeth of sensible counsels against the idea. The Merchant's own views are expressed with an **irony** obvious to his listeners, but not to himself: 'A man may do no synne with his wfy/Ne hurte hymselven with his owene knyf' (II. 1839–40). We get little insight into May. The Merchant describes the garden where she commits adultery more vividly than he describes her. He discredits her through fleeting images – as when she throws her love-letter into the privy – but denies her the internal monologues he gives Januarie. Instead of a stage filled with complex characters affecting and changing one another, we have a portrait built up in layers, each taking us deeper into the heart of one man.

CRITICAL INTERPRETATIONS

Performance history

The first production

The first production of *A Doll's House* in Copenhagen in 1879 appropriately took place on 21 December, the longest night of the year. It starred Betty Hennings, much loved for playing dizzy young women. Her Nora was above all a child, high-spirited and physically lively. Hennings was a former ballerina. Her brilliant tarantella not only expressed Nora's mental turmoil but suggested the talents and energies she might discover in her new life. Critics were universal in their praise for the way she handled the transition to the more sober figure of the last act. However, Ibsen's friend, the critic Georg Brandes, also considered that there was a dimension missing – the physical passion that made the break-up truly poignant.

Nora appealed to the imagination of critics, and they were prepared to debate aspects of her character. However, they were puzzled by some of the other performances, suggesting that they had made up their minds before the play began. Helmer was the focus of much sympathy; they felt he had a lot to put up with. Emil Poulsen courageously played Helmer without any attempt to court such sympathy. He was promptly dismissed as 'coarse' by several critics, including Herman Bang. Krogstad was almost universally seen as a villain, and most early Krogstads had to struggle against playing to confirm the preconception.

Victorian England

In England the role of Nora was the undisputed property of Janet Achurch, who financed the 1889 production. She was a close friend of Shaw, sharing his interest in Ibsen as a social radical. He described her as 'the only tragic actress of genius we now possess' (Bernard Ince, *Before Ibsen: the early stage career of Janet Achurch, 1883-89, Theatre Notebook* (Volume 67 no. 2, 2013). Over the years her interpretation of Nora increasingly drew on this tragic aspect. Originally full of childish fun, like Betty Hennings, in her later career she gave the role a wild, bitter strength. Her reviewers always perceived her performance as a very special theatrical event. What they praised was not so much the way she tackled specific lines, but the intelligence with which she approached the play.

Her performance always offered something to discuss after the fall of the curtain – perhaps the main source of enjoyment for the early audiences of the play. Hostile critics complained of 'its almost total lack of dramatic action' (*The Times*, 8 June 1889). Achurch, however, felt that the audience should be free to judge the rights and wrongs of Nora's action. Her chief concern was that they should appreciate the realities of her situation and she felt that the ideas expressed in the final discussion made the ending dramatically exciting. Her performance of the last scene in 1897, with Courtenay Thorpe as Helmer, brought about a powerful curtain appreciated even by the Ibsen-hating Clement Scott: 'The acting was so good that, if we may express it so, the man becomes the hysterical woman, and the woman becomes the silent, sullen, and determined man' (*Daily Telegraph*, 11 May 1897).

KEY INTERPRETATION

One of the most enthusiastically received productions of the last twenty years was Anthony Page's at the Belasco, New York, in 1997. This explored the silly and girlish aspects of Nora in a new way. Janet McTeer's mannered style suggested a comic actress beginning to realise her part was unworthy of her, trying silly voices and gestures with a slightly hopeless air. Between husband and wife was a strong sexual bond that made the final parting agonising. McTeer's Nora struggled to articulate what she had discovered about herself, reborn intellectually even as she was tearing herself away.

KEY INTERPRETATION A05

Hattie Morahan's Nora abandoned many of Nora's soliloquies; instead, we could see glimpses of life in other rooms which added to the sense of pressure on Nora by never letting her be fully alone. In contrast, Cush Jumbo in Greg Hersov's 2013 production for Manchester Royal Exchange, a theatre in the round, used her proximity to the audience to speak directly to them. It may be helpful to consider what you as an audience member might gain from either approach.

Twentieth-century approaches

As social changes deprived the play of much of its shock value, many directors abandoned **naturalism** and used new images and designs to explore the characters' personal conflicts. In 1972, Hans Neuenfels produced it in Stuttgart as a story about a failure of communication. The characters moved like puppets with invisible strings, turning to the audience rather than to one another as if it was a waste of time trying to gain understanding within the marriage. Even the children were not addressed directly. The figure of the nurse haunted Nora throughout, softly repeating the word 'duty', like her own emerging consciousness. At the beginning Nora lay on the sofa while Helmer loomed up through a window wearing the bowler hat of a banker. At the end he lay on the sofa, arms outstretched as if crucified, the victim of his conformist society rather than an agent of it. Nora appeared above his head through the window.

In 1989, Ingmar Bergman stripped the play of Victoriana and set it in a box lined with red velvet, without doors or windows. Rather than allowing the action to flow, he divided it into separate scenes. Each was played with a single, symbolic piece of furniture. At first the tree, and the dolls and toys around it, suggested that Nora and Helmer inhabited a playpen. Later, the final, painful parting was staged on a vast brass bed. The emphasis was not so much on the liberation of Nora as on the way the other characters act as her mirrors. All the actors remained on stage throughout, quietly seated on chairs at the side, and stepped forward on cue.

Contemporary productions

A Doll's House has seen some notable recent revivals. Carrie Cracknell's production for the Young Vic in 2012 (see below) laid a new stress on Nora's sheer terror. The audience could see all the rooms in the small apartment on a revolving set. Hattie Morahan's Nora moved within it like a caged mouse on a wheel. Her most relaxed moments, with her children, including a small baby, were sharply cut off by the new fear that she was failing as a mother. Her tarantella was accompanied by swooping, sinister music that suggested the noise in Nora's own head as she danced to a twitching standstill like one of the poison victims for whom the dance is named.

As Helmer began his speech on forgiveness, the set revolved to allow a glimpse of the bedroom. She slowly moved there and began to put on dark items of clothing, almost ritualistically, before he entered the room for the final confrontation sitting on the bed. Her stark disillusion turned to rage – on the words 'I'm a human being' she struck Helmer as he tried to grasp her; the anger escalated as she began to realise just how far society, as well as her husband, had failed her.

Early critical responses

First spectators

Early European responses to *A Doll's House* focused on its ending. **Idealists** and churchmen were divided. Some wanted a noble and maternal Nora to give the audience something to aspire to. Some complained that Ibsen's Nora was unrealistic because real women *were* noble and maternal. After the Copenhagen premiere the critic M. W. Brun stated that any real wife would 'throw herself into her husband's arms', and maintained that the play's 'screaming dissonances' defied common sense (*Folkets Avis* 24 December 1879). Fredrik Petersen, a theologian at the University of Kristiania, declared that the lack of a reconciliation scene was a serious flaw. He found the play 'ugly' and 'distressing' (*Aftenbladet*, January 1880).

In Germany, Ibsen was accused of 'loving the repulsive', and the ending of *A Doll's House* was called 'illogical and immoral' (quoted in Michael Meyer, *Ibsen*, 1985, p. 482). Such views were countered by radical left-wing critics who felt that 'our own life, our own everyday life, has here been placed on stage and condemned!' (quoted in Moi, *Henrik Ibsen and the Birth of Modernism*, 2006, p. 228). But though delighted by the energy of the play, they largely discussed it as an attack on marriage; its theatrical complexity and innovation tended to be ignored.

British critics

Clement Scott, Ibsen's most implacable enemy in England, centred his attack on Nora's personality. He assumed, without question, that this was inherent rather than formed by her circumstances, demanding: 'How Torvald Helmer could by any possibility have treated his restless, illogical, fractious and babyish little wife otherwise than he did; why Nora should ever adore with such abandonment and passion this conceited prig … are points that … require a considerable amount of argument … to convince the common-sense playgoer' (*Daily Telegraph*, 8 June 1889). The *Spectator* acknowledged what it termed Ibsen's 'useful lesson' that treating women as children leads to 'distorted relations'. However, it complained of a 'moral vacuum' at the end, blaming Nora for her unwillingness to 'make a hero where she had failed to find one' (*Spectator*, 21 June 1889).

British supporters

One of the most substantial pro-Ibsen manifestos was George Bernard Shaw's *The Quintessence of Ibsenism* (1891). What Shaw, like many of his contemporaries in the socialist and suffragist movements, most admired in Ibsen was his 'sharpshooting at the audience' (*The Quintessence of Ibsenism*, 1932 edition, p. 63). Eleanor Marx valued Nora as a woman of adult moral stature. She complained that critical discussion of *A Doll's House* was distorted by a particularly English narrowness which perceived the word 'morality' as 'like the word 'virtue' … applied to only one special quality … sexual relations' (*Time,* March 1891).

Revision task 10: A controversial play A01

George Bernard Shaw published two volumes of Ibsen-influenced plays which he called *Plays Pleasant* and *Plays Unpleasant*. In which volume would you put *A Doll's House?* Write short notes giving your reasons.

Later critical approaches

Ibsen's reputation wanes

Despite the fact that *A Doll's House* is one of the most frequently performed plays in the world, Ibsen's work has suffered from a lack of critical reappraisal. For a long time, he was only discussed as a **naturalist**, although his work explores a number of different styles. By the end of the Second World War naturalism itself was called into question. The influential German critic and philosopher Theodor W. Adorno (1903–69) noted that Ibsen's very name induced boredom. The playwright and his plays both seemed 'outdated' (quoted in Toril Moi's *Henrik Ibsen and the Birth of Modernism: Art, Theater, Philosophy*, 2006, p. 18).

The most thoughtful twentieth-century English critic of Ibsen, the Marxist Raymond Williams, complained that 'Ibsen and Stanislavsky have won' (*Drama from Ibsen to Brecht*, 1976, p. 7). By this Williams meant that Ibsen had outlived his usefulness. It had been important for him to show the psychological and political limitations of bourgeois domestic life, but the theatre now needed to move on. Williams's *Drama from Ibsen to Brecht* locates the future of drama in theatrical techniques that do not disguise their artificiality but embrace it.

Others complained that Ibsen was not naturalistic *enough*. They felt the structure of the earlier plays was too obvious in comparison with later writers. Ronald Gray's *Ibsen: A Dissenting View* (1977) makes this accusation at length, accusing *A Doll's House* of cynically exploiting the techniques of popular drama.

Beyond naturalism

Recent critics, who value a variety of different theatrical traditions, consider that what makes *A Doll's House* interesting is precisely its non-naturalistic elements. In 2006 Toril Moi offered the most radical reappraisal of Ibsen since Williams, in *Henrik Ibsen and the Birth of Modernism*. She sees Ibsen as part of the **modernist** movement, which demanded new forms to fit a changing world in all the arts, whether music, painting, novels and poetry or architecture. Ibsen, who had wanted to be a painter and had written poetry and philosophical essays, drew on all these disciplines. He was less interested in trying to provide a photographic image of real life than in critiquing the false and strained images of idealist drama.

Moi pays equal attention to plays like *A Doll's House,* which preserve a realistic surface, and the more poetic and symbolic plays. She compares him, for instance, to writers such as Oscar Wilde and James Joyce, who tested the limits of existing forms. Ibsen's lively treatment of 'theatricality' in *A Doll's House* shows the limits of the **well-made play** even while keeping its structure. Helmer sneers at Nora's 'melodrama' but is busily acting out a theatrical stereotype of masculinity even as he speaks. Nora uses theatricality as a way to hide from reality, but also to express herself, as she does in the tarantella. *A Doll's House*, Moi suggests, is an 'invitation to reflect on the nature of theatre' (*Henrik Ibsen and the Birth of Modernism*, 2006, p. 237).

Feminist readings

Ibsen's remark that he had not consciously 'worked in the interests of the woman-question' (Robert Ferguson, *Henrik Ibsen*, Richard Cohen Books, London, 1996, p. 39) has sometimes been taken too literally – although he liked to provoke and irritate. Over the years this has given rise to the idea that the women's movement somehow imposed a false reading, and that *A Doll's House* is 'nothing to do with the sexes' (Michael Meyer, *Henrik Ibsen, The Farewell to Poetry*, Granada, 1971, p. 266). In the late 1990s feminist critics began to debate this.

Alisa Solomon suggests that the generalisation comes from a failure to realise how innovative Ibsen was as a naturalistic writer. She shows in great detail the exact environment that determines the circumstances that make women like Nora what they are – including those details which would only be there in the case of a woman (*Re-Dressing the Canon*, Routledge, 1997). Solomon goes on to ask, if characters like Nora are appreciated as **metaphors** for the human condition, male or female, what it is that makes them so. Her conclusion is that it is the 'theatricality' that informs Nora's character. To be a woman is to be expected to play a series of roles – the devoted mother, the helpless heroine who needs to be rescued, the seductive charmer. This is equally true of the nineteenth-century woman and the heroine of the well-made play. Nora performs all these as expected. However, at the end of the play she has to create a new role for herself. Ibsen 'reveals the artificiality of the well-made play, and … the artificiality of the well-made woman'.

A03 KEY CONTEXT

The expatriate Irish writer James Joyce is famed for his radically new treatment of human consciousness, at its most experimental in the highly controversial *Finnegans Wake* (1939). His novel *Ulysses* (1922), the short-story collection *Dubliners* (1914) and the autobiographical *A Portrait of the Artist as a Young Man* (1914–15) all show characters, like Nora, at odds with the world they live in and needing to break free. A good linguist, in 1901 Joyce wrote an admiring letter in Dano-Norwegian to Ibsen.

A01 PROGRESS BOOSTER

Alisa Solomon makes the point that the early interpreters of Nora, such as Janet Achurch, were a new kind of performer. Rather than coming from theatrical acting dynasties, they had a broad education and were politically active. As she puts it, to play the 'new woman' it was necessary to create a 'new actress' (*Re-Dressing the Canon*, p. 51). You may find it helpful to think about what qualities might be needed to interpret Nora on stage.

Feminist influences

In *Ibsen's Women* (Plunket Lake Press, 2015), Joan Templeton takes issue with the assumption that the plays can only be 'universal' if they ignore the feminist energies both in them and around their creation. She explored Ibsen's personal papers to uncover the lively intellectual friendships Ibsen maintained with feminist thinkers of his day. These included his wife, his mother-in-law, and the actresses who created his characters. She finds his plays to be imbued with their ideas and their personalities, and notes, 'The power of *A Doll's House* lies not beyond but in its feminism.'

The play on stage

The end of the twentieth century also marked an interest in what can be learned about Ibsen from the theatre. Frederick J. Marker and Lise-Lone Marker, in *Ibsen's Lively Art: A Performance Study of the Major Plays* (1989), start from the idea that a play can only be fully understood as an encounter between the performer and the audience. They see the work of designers, directors and actors as an 'essential dimension' (p. ix.) of studying Ibsen. His strength lies in the number of possibilities it opens up for creative response. They note that Nora particularly sets the performer free to develop and innovate. One chapter is specifically about 'One Nora, many Noras'.

Contemporary approaches

Marxist criticism

Marxism poses certain basic questions about society: Who has the power? Who makes a profit? At whose expense do they make it? When watching a play, a Marxist critic might ask these questions about the characters within it. They might also ask questions about the writer and the theatre that produced the play: Does the play question the society it is set in? Whose story has the writer chosen to tell? Is it being told at the expense of someone of a lower financial or social status?

Helmer is a member of the bourgeoisie, the class which controls the means of producing wealth and which coerces others to produce that wealth. As a banker and a former lawyer he is the most powerful figure in the play. Although we do not see the powerful people who control him in turn – those who make the law, or own the bank – we know that he is afraid of them. His terror of what people might think of him means that when he exercises power over people like Krogstad his actions are shaped by fear.

Nora, as a bourgeois wife, is the focus of the play. This means that we only see the other women of the Helmer household, the maid and the nurse, in relation to her. We must assume they have stories of their own. However, the maid exists as a narrative convenience. We do not know how she feels about admitting suspicious characters like Krogstad, carrying letters on bank business at short notice, or even about being woken in the middle of the night to present a letter on a tray to Nora. We know a little of the nurse's story, but we have no idea what will happen to her at the end of the play.

Nora goes off to become an individual. We assume from her conversation with Mrs Linde about work that she aspires to become part of the petite bourgeoisie, the class which does not control society but supports the structure that does. She will not be rich but she will earn sufficient money, leisure and status to have the luxury of forging a personal identity. This is to some extent at the expense of the nurse and those of her class. These people keep the social structure afloat by offering essential services, for which they do not receive enough money to enjoy the same opportunities for personal growth.

Marxist feminism

Marxist feminists have turned their attention to the way women themselves can be turned into commodities, or **reified**. This has certainly happened to the nurse, Nora and Mrs Linde. Nora may well have been Helmer's reward for helping her father. Eventually she describes her marriage as if she were an object, 'passed from papa's hands into yours' (Act Three, p. 98). Although Helmer's nicknames suggestive of household pets make it clear that he sees Nora as a possession, this process of reification is not something of which he is consciously aware.

Mrs Linde is quite clear in her mind that she has been an object of exchange – she sold herself to a rich husband in order to keep herself and her family. Krogstad expresses bitterness about this fact, but only because he himself suffered as a result. He does not criticise society for allowing such transactions to take place. Nora, however, does. She is not yet confident enough to say 'which is right, society or I' (Act Three, p. 101) but she is no longer an object. She is a subject, who can both learn and speak about what she has learned to others.

Gendered criticism

A Doll's House remains one of the most powerful refutations ever written of the theory of separate spheres. The nineteenth century considered that men and women belonged in the workplace and the home respectively – but these spheres were not exactly equal. Feminist critics have pointed out that masculinity has often been associated with light, goodness and culture; femininity with darkness, evil and untamed nature – that is, it is something to be fought and defeated.

In contrast, Judith Butler's *Gender Trouble: Feminism and the Subversion of Identity* (1990) suggests that there is no such thing as innate masculinity or femininity. Rather, our gender (not our biological sex) is not something we *are*, but something we *do*. Society for many years has assumed that certain kinds of behaviour are 'natural'. For men, these include working for money, fighting and social control. For women, they involve childbearing, nurturing and submissively pleasing men.

Nineteenth-century costumes make this very apparent. Men dressed plainly, fitting their role as working breadwinners; beards and moustaches stressed their unlikeness to women. The clothes of even moderately well-to-do women were elaborate, emphasising the small waist and large hips that the period considered 'feminine'. Nora is a fashionable dresser and probably conforms to this style – and her Capri dress, chosen by Helmer, will reflect his taste.

 KEY INTERPRETATION

In 2009, Kfir Yefet's production of *A Doll's House* at the Donmar Warehouse shifted the action to Edwardian London. In Zinnie Harris's free new translation, Helmer became Thomas Vaughan, an ambitious new cabinet minister who proclaims to his wife, 'Our staple is trust; it's all we have to offer the public'. The change made it easier for the audience to appreciate what was at stake – a bank manager no longer has to worry about his reputation to the extent Helmer does, but a politician might still credibly consider his image to be very fragile.

A05 **KEY INTERPRETATION**

The novelist A. S. Byatt, reviewing Gillian Anderson's performance in *A Doll's House* at the Donmar Warehouse in 2009 (see photo, left), points out that the originality of the play lies in the way we do not necessarily like or admire Nora, but can still be moved by the choice she makes: 'Great tragedy asks us to care for flawed or even stupid people … but the glory of *A Doll's House* is that it asks us to care for a small-minded person, in the moment of her realisation of her own small-mindedness.' (*The Guardian*, 2 May 2009)

In her 2014 production of *A Doll's House* at the Belvoir Theatre Upstairs in Sydney, the writer and director Anne-Louise Sarks continued the story, following Nora through the door and into her new world. She comments, 'The things that hold Nora back in 2014 aren't as obvious but they are just as insidious. I wanted to shine a light on the personal inside the political ... This play asks us who we are and who we want to be. And it demands we ask that of our most personal selves too.' (Belvoir St. website)

Both Nora and Helmer can be seen determinedly performing their gender stereotypes. We see her play the submissive and cajoling wife flattering Helmer into giving Mrs Linde a job, as if work was something for 'clever' people, not her (Act One, p. 41). Helmer tells Nora, 'I would not be a true man if your feminine helplessness did not make you doubly attractive in my eyes' and offers her the protection of his 'wings' like some masculine divinity (Act Three, pp. 95–6.) Both of them literally dress up in order to express their stereotypes more clearly. Nora dresses as the peasant dancing for Helmer's pleasure; he becomes the master of the dance in a cloak which suggests his 'wings'. Both indulge in the language of **melodrama**, a genre which deals in strong heroes and helpless heroines.

By the end of the play Nora at least can see these roles as demeaning and corrupting – just as she has ceased to divide people into 'us' and 'strangers'. She has tried out, and liked, the role of breadwinner, more conventionally associated with men. Helmer does not yet know how to be different. For instance, he reproaches Nora with her duty to 'her' children. However, he has no real interaction with them in the play. His 'maternal' side is completely absent. It is for the audience to decide whether it is possible for Helmer and Nora to make a marriage that permits a more free performance of gender roles. As Toril Moi writes, 'What will it take for two modern individuals to build a relationship ...based on freedom, equality and love?' (*Henrik Ibsen and the Birth of Modernism: Art, Theater, Philosophy*, 2006, p. 147).

Performance criticism

Performance study is a relatively new field, one which underlines that there is no definitive reading of a play. The insights of the actors, the director, the designer and members of the public for a single performance offer a unique understanding. The more productions you see, the more possibilities you can find in a text. You will also be able to see how a performance illuminates its own time.

The most recent text on performance criticism to explore *A Doll's House* is Frode Helland's *Ibsen in Performance* (Bloomsbury, 2015). She goes beyond the Markers' focus on Western theatre (see **Later critical approaches**) and examines the relationship of Ibsen's plays to other cultural traditions at different points in time. In doing so she discovers new readings and also explains how the meaning of the play varies in different contexts.

Thomas Ostermeier's 2003 production of *A Doll's House* saw Nora and Helmer as inhabiting a consumerist, money-obsessed world. The play was set in a beautifully stylish upper-middle-class home like an illustration to a lifestyle magazine. Nora did not merely slam the door. She shot Helmer.

Two performances

Frode Helland explores two productions in Chile. The first was in 1980, at the Catholic University, using period sets and costumes and taking no liberties with the text. However, new plays had been forbidden under the regime of General Pinochet; 'classic' plays were the only way to comment on the situation. Nora's desire to speak her mind and ask questions in the face of Helmer's belittling behaviour was seen as a courageous defence of free speech. One critic claimed that Nora represented 'the entire Chilean people' (*Ibsen in Practice*, 2015, p. 51).

In contrast, a version played in Santiago in 2012 by Teatro la Maria, a group led by Alexandra von Hummel and Alexias Moreno, entitled *In Pursuit of Nora Helmer,* stressed that although the repressive regime was over, society was dominated by male language and attitudes. The play opened with five figures in silhouette; all of them were wearing short skirts and high heels. As the lights went up, three of them were revealed to be male. As the play progressed, the actors playing male roles grew more emphatically masculine in their manner. It became clear that although women were now free to suggest that gender roles were social constructs, in practice the power remained with men. In the final scene, Helmer appeared in full male dress to utter his most repressive lines.

The play in the world

Over the last decades it has been possible to see a Nora singing a song from the Chinese Opera, a Helmer dancing with his male friends, a Nora who leaves with her daughter. Since 2008, the Norwegian Government has awarded 'Ibsen scholarships' for projects all over the world: so far, *A Doll's House* has generated the most. A new play by the Egyptian writer-director Nora Amin, *Nora's Doors,* showed five women and their different reasons for walking through the same door. *Nora Nure*, by Theatre Painted Bird, combined the story of Nora with a Kurdish folk tale. The story of the woman who slammed the door has gone far beyond her origins to inspire theatrical and social change.

 KEY INTERPRETATION

The critic Andrew Dickson, introducing Ibsen on the Barbican website, suggests that British productions of *A Doll's House* have failed to move with the times: 'The lingering effects of Stanislavskian realism, not to mention a *Downton*-like taste for period detail, have made his plays seem more about the dangers of excessive crinoline- and frockcoat-wearing than anything more politically pertinent. Otherwise fine British productions of *A Doll's House* – and there have been many – are swaddled in chintz and antimacassars, as if Ibsen were Julian Fellowes in angrier, Nordic form.'

PROGRESS CHECK

Section One: Check your understanding

These tasks will help you to evaluate your knowledge and skills level in this particular area.

1. Choose a section from a work from a different period which explores the nature of marriage. Compare it with *A Doll's House* and list the differences you notice.

2. What do we know about Helmer's economic status in his world? Write a short report.

3. What challenges would the play offer a nineteenth-century actress? Make a short list.

4. Who would you describe as the most powerful character in the play? List your reasons.

5. How is the Norwegian setting important to the action? List your ideas.

6. How might an adaptation of the play tell you something about the period that produced it?

7. Compare two different critical views and say which you agree with most. List your reasons.

8. List the women in the play in order of social power, with reasons. Put your ideas in a two-column table.

9. Look at a review of the play from the nineteenth century. What does the reviewer take for granted about the relationships between men and women? Make a brief list. [See left for a possible extract you could use as the basis for your response.]

10. At what points in the play do you think Nora and Helmer conform most closely to the gender roles their society endorses? Make a brief list.

Section Two: Working towards the exam

Choose one of the following three tasks which require longer, more developed answers.

1. 'A Doll's House is the first truly modern play about marriage.' Do you find it 'modern'? Give your reasons for or against.

2. 'All the relationships in the play are based in some way upon economic power.' Do you agree? Give reasons for or against.

3. 'Helmer is nothing but a collection of stereotypes of masculinity.' Do you agree? List your reasons for or against and suggest how this might affect the actor's performance.

KEY INTERPRETATION

Extract from M. V. Brun's review of the first performance in 1879, in the Danish magazine *Folkets Avis*:

'..all the enjoyment [Ibsen] offers us in the first acts, evaporates in the third, and we are left there in the most embarrassing ambience, almost revoltingly affected by a catastrophe, which in the crassest way breaks with the common human qualities to celebrate the untrue, the in every aesthetic, psychological and dramatic respect distressing.'

PROGRESS BOOSTER

For each Section Two task, read the question carefully, select the key areas you need to address, and plan an essay of six to seven points. Write a first draft, giving yourself an hour to do so. Make sure you include supporting evidence for each point, including quotations.

Progress check (rate your understanding on a level of 1 – low, to 5 – high)	1	2	3	4	5
How some knowledge of context enhances interpretation of the play					
The different ways the play can be read, according to critical approaches such as feminist or Marxist					
How comparison with another literary work can deepen understanding of both					
How a reader's interpretation may differ from the author's intended meaning					
How *A Doll's House* can be read as a historical document					

ASSESSMENT FOCUS

How will you be assessed?

Each particular exam board and exam paper will be slightly different, so make sure you check with your teacher exactly which Assessment Objectives you need to focus on. For example, on AQA/B you are likely to get more marks for Assessment Objectives 1, 2 and 3, but this does not mean you should discount 4 or 5, while AO2 is not assessed by OCR in relation to *A Doll's House*. Bear in mind that if you are doing AS Level, although the weightings are the same, there will be no coursework element.

What do the AOs actually mean?

Assessment Objective	Meaning?
AO1 Articulate informed, personal and creative responses to literary texts, using associated concepts and terminology, and coherent, accurate written expression.	You write about texts in accurate, clear and precise ways so that what you have to say is clear to the marker. You use literary terms (e.g. **comedy**) or refer to concepts (e.g. **metatheatre**) in relevant places. You do not simply repeat what you have read or been told, but express your own ideas based on in-depth knowledge of the text and related issues.
AO2 Analyse ways in which meanings are shaped in literary texts.	You are able to explain in detail how the specific techniques and methods used by Ibsen to create the text (e.g. characterisation, dialogue, **metaphor**) influence and affect the reader's response.
AO3 Demonstrate understanding of the significance and influence of the contexts in which literary texts are written and received.	You can explain how the text might reflect the social, historical, political or personal backgrounds of Ibsen or the time when the play was written. You also consider how *A Doll's House* might have been received differently over time.
AO4 Explore connections across literary texts.	You are able to explain links between the *A Doll's House* and other texts, perhaps of a similar genre, or with similar concerns (e.g. *Madame Bovary*), or viewed from a similar perspective (e.g. Marxist).
AO5 Explore literary texts informed by different interpretations.	You understand how *A Doll's House* can be viewed in different ways, and are able to write about these debates, forming your own opinion. For example, how a critic might view Helmer as the real villain of the play, while another might see him as, like Nora, a victim of gender stereotyping.

What does this mean for your revision?

Whether you are following an AS or A Level course, use the right-hand column above to measure how confidently you can address these objectives. Then focus your revision on those aspects you feel need most attention. Remember, throughout these Notes, the AOs are highlighted, so you can flick through and check them in that way.

Next, use the tables on pages 86 and 87. These help you understand the differences between a satisfactory and an outstanding response.

Then, use the guidance from page 88 onwards to help you address the key AOs, for example how to shape and plan your writing.

Features of **mid-level** responses: the following examples relate to the role of Dr Rank in the play.

	Features	Examples
AO1	You use critical vocabulary appropriately for most of the time, and your arguments are relevant to the task, ordered sensibly, with clear expression. You show detailed knowledge of the text.	*Rank initially appears to be the play's **raisonneur** – a sympathetic and wise, but essentially detached, **observer who comments on the action**.*
AO2	You show straightforward understanding of the writer's methods, such as how form, structure and language shape meanings.	*Ibsen is **exploring the theme of heredity in the play**. Rank is not like his dissolute father; although she is called a 'spendthrift', Nora has not inherited her father's carelessness with money. The way Ibsen **sets up parallels between characters** like this help us to understand Nora. They also make the point that 'society', despite Nora calling it 'a bore', is important. **Everybody in the play is linked to everyone else.**''*
AO3	You can write about a range of contextual factors and make some relevant links between these and the task or text.	*Rank, and Nora, repeatedly talk about death. He will die shortly after his last appearance; she will survive and grow and change. **Ibsen and his contemporaries were very affected by Darwinism,** which is concerned with the survival of the species. Nora is becoming a new kind of person, one needed if the human race is to develop and progress. Rank shows this when he thanks her for the 'light'.*
AO4	You consider straightforward connections between texts and write about them clearly and relevantly to the task.	*Rank's hereditary illness allows us to consider whether people are shaped by heredity or free to change. **Ibsen developed the idea in his next play, 'Ghosts'.** The central character, Oswald, knows his mind will suffer as inherited syphilis takes hold. His mother, **unlike Nora**, chose to stay in her loveless marriage. **Both plays ask us to think about responsibility and also forgiveness:** Rank is tolerant when he speaks of his father.*
AO5	You tackle the debate in the task in a clear, logical way, showing your understanding of different interpretations.	***Some early critics argued that Dr Rank's role was irrelevant – 'The Times' review of the first British production called him 'incidental'.** This is perhaps because they were shocked by Nora even contemplating asking a man for money and were not interested in what the man was like. **However, Rank is important to Nora's moral growth** throughout the play. He is the only person to treat her as an adult, and **she comes to her first really adult decision when she decides not to involve him in her debts.***

Features of a **high-level** response: these examples relate to a task on theatrical perspectives.

	Features	Examples
A01	You are perceptive, and assured in your argument in relation to the task. You make fluent, confident use of literary concepts and terminology; and express yourself confidently.	*Like many plays, 'A Doll's House' focuses on the experience of one character, but **we see it through many lenses**: through what the character says, and what is said of the character; through action, expressed in the **stage directions;** through the **set;** through the **theatrical conventions** used (and arguably, in this case, challenged) by the playwright.*
A02	You explore and analyse key aspects of Ibsen's use of form, structure and language and evaluate perceptively how they shape meanings.	*The beginning, with Nora hiding her macaroons and showing off gifts, suggests a **domestic comedy**. As the blackmail plot develops it resembles **melodrama**: Nora's wilder **soliloquies,** her dance, the way she snatches up Helmer's coat intending to rush out into the night in Act Three, all fit its **conventions**. However, Ibsen undercuts these devices – most notably with Helmer's selfish rejoicing after the paper is returned and Nora's disillusion with her hero. The play is not a **melodrama** but a **critique** of the gender stereotypes in which melodrama is grounded.*
A03	You show deep, detailed and relevant understanding of how contextual factors link to the text or task.	*While the imaginations of Nora and Helmer are shaped by these expectations, the play offers the audience alternative images, which are explored in a **naturalistic** style. For example, we are invited to consider the enterprise of the New Woman, represented by Mrs Linde, as another possible identity for Nora.*
A04	You show a detailed and perceptive understanding of issues raised through connections between texts. You have a range of excellent supportive references.	***Comedy,*** *such as 'The Importance of Being Earnest', ends with the integration of characters into their world, generally by marriage;* ***tragedy,*** *such as 'Death of a Salesman', ends with the disintegration of an individual at odds with their society. 'A Doll's House' does not have a conclusive ending like this: it ends with characters in transition. We are not asked to mourn or to celebrate, but to think.*
A05	You are able to use your knowledge of critical debates and the possible perspectives on an issue to write fluently and confidently about how the text might be interpreted.	*In **Marxist-feminist** terms, Nora has become **'commodified'**, reduced to an object bartered by her father for Helmer's silence before the play begins. Her struggle is not ultimately about being blackmailed by Krogstad as much as about reaching this insight and forging an independent identity (part of which involves financial independence).*

HOW TO WRITE HIGH-QUALITY RESPONSES

The quality of your writing – how you express your ideas – is vital for getting a higher grade, and **AO1** and **AO2** are specifically about **how** you respond.

Five key areas

The quality of your responses can be broken down into **five** key areas.

1. The structure of your answer/essay

- First, get **straight to the point in your opening paragraph**. Use a sharp, direct first sentence that deals with a key aspect and then follow up with evidence or detailed reference.
- **Put forward an argument or point of view** (you won't **always** be able to challenge or take issue with the essay question, but generally, where you can, you are more likely to write in an interesting way).
- **Signpost your ideas** with connectives and references which help the essay flow. Aim to present an overall argument or conceptual response to the task, not a series of unconnected points.
- **Don't repeat points already made**, not even in the conclusion, unless you have something new to add.

Aiming high: Effective opening paragraphs

Let's imagine you have been asked about the roles of women in the play.

Here's an example of a successful opening paragraph:

> Gets straight to the point

> 'A Doll's House' was a key text for the emerging feminist movement of the nineteenth century because it offers not just one image of female freedom but the sense of multiple possibilities. In the course of the action Nora and Mrs Linde both re-define themselves, in completely different ways. Nora escapes a suffocating stereotype of feminine helplessness, which she has hitherto felt obliged to act out, and elects to 'try and become' a 'human being'. Mrs Linde opts for a more conventional role as homemaker, but achieves it through radically unconventional actions.

> Sets up some interesting ideas that will be tackled in subsequent paragraphs

2. Use of titles, names, etc.

This is a simple, but important, tip to stay on the right side of the examiners.

- Make sure that you spell correctly the titles of the texts, chapters, authors and so on. Present them correctly too, with inverted commas and capitals as appropriate. For example, In 'A Doll's House' ....
- Use the **full title**, unless there is a good reason not to (e.g. it's very long).
- Use the term 'text' rather than 'book' or 'story'. If you use the word 'story', the examiner may **think you mean the** plot/action rather than the 'text' as a whole.

3. Effective quotations

Do not 'bolt on' quotations to the points you make. You will get some marks for including them, but examiners will not find your writing very fluent.

The best quotations are:

- Relevant and not too long (you are going to have to memorise them, so that will help you select shorter ones!)
- Integrated into your argument/sentence
- Linked to effect and implications

Aiming high: Effective use of quotations

Here is an example of an effective use of a quotation about social class in the play:

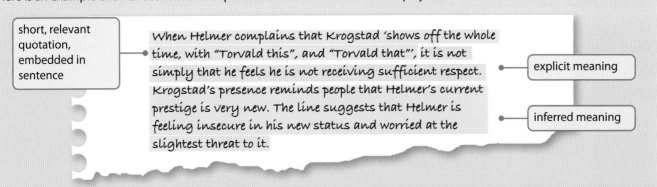

| short, relevant quotation, embedded in sentence |
| explicit meaning |
| inferred meaning |

When Helmer complains that Krogstad 'shows off the whole time, with "Torvald this", and "Torvald that"', it is not simply that he feels he is not receiving sufficient respect. Krogstad's presence reminds people that Helmer's current prestige is very new. The line suggests that Helmer is feeling insecure in his new status and worried at the slightest threat to it.

Remember – quotations can be one or two single words or phrases embedded in a sentence to build a picture or explanation, or they can be longer ones that are explored and picked apart.

4. Techniques and terminology

By all means mention literary terms, techniques, conventions, critical theories or people (for example, 'paradox', 'archetype', 'feminism' or 'Stanislavsky') **but** make sure that you:

- Understand what they mean
- Are able to link them to what you're saying
- Spell them correctly

5. General writing skills

Try to write in a way that sounds professional and uses standard English. This does not mean that your writing will lack personality – just that it will be authoritative.

- Avoid colloquial or everyday expressions such as 'got', 'alright', 'ok' and so on.
- Use terms such as 'convey', 'suggest', 'imply', 'infer' to explain the writer's methods.
- Refer to 'we' when discussing the audience/reader.
- Avoid assertions and generalisations; don't just state a general point of view (' Nora becomes more aware of society as the play goes on'), but analyse closely with clear evidence and textual detail.

Note the professional approach here in the choice of vocabulary and awareness of the effect on the reader:

Ibsen conveys the sense of a society in flux, changed unrecognisably by industrialisation and by new political and social ideas. As an audience we are made aware of these through the presence of Mrs Linde, an image of the New Woman.

EXAMINER'S TIP

It's important to remember that *A Doll's House* is a text created by Henrik Ibsen – thinking about the choices Ibsen makes with language and plotting will not only alert you to his methods as a playwright but also his intentions, i.e. the effect he seeks to create.

QUESTIONS WITH STATEMENTS, QUOTATIONS OR VIEWPOINTS

EXAMINER'S TIP

Often students are set a question on one particular aspect (such as Nora's development) but end up writing almost as much about another (such as the relationship between Nora and Helmer). They are answering the question they would like to have seen! **Stick to the question set**, and answer **all parts of it**.

One type of question you may come across is one that includes a statement, quotation or viewpoint from another reader. You are likely to be asked this about *A Doll's House* and another text you have studied, but it won't be a comparison, so we will deal just with *A Doll's House* here.

These questions ask you to respond to, or argue for/against, a specific **point of view** or critical interpretation.

For *A Doll's House* these questions will typically be like this:

> *'A Doll's House* is not a tragedy but a comedy about a serious issue.' To what extent do you agree with this view? Remember to include in your answer relevant detailed exploration of Ibsen's dramatic methods.

The key thing to remember is that you are being asked to **respond to a particular perspective or critical view** of the text – in other words, to come up with **your own** 'take' on the idea or viewpoint in the task.

Key skills required

The table below provides help and advice on answering the question above.

Skill	Means?	How do I achieve this?
To focus on the specific aspect, by exploring Ibsen's dramatic methods	You must show your understanding of comedy as a genre and how a writer might use comic techniques in a play that is not in itself a comedy.	You will need to deal with the issue generally, either in an opening paragraph or in several paragraphs, but also make sure you keep on coming back to this issue throughout the essay, rather than diverting into other areas which you have not been asked about.
To consider different interpretations	There will be more than one way of looking at the given question. For example, critics might be divided about the extent to which the characters suffer – for instance, Stanley Fish famously wrote that the final scene should be 'harrowing' because Helmer's love is real.	Show you have considered these different interpretations in your answer. For example, a student might write: *In comedy, characters often go through painful experiences, but they learn from them and survive. In the last scene Nora has learned to see life beyond gender stereotypes; Helmer has at least been made aware this is possible. As with many comedies, a lesson has been learned and the characters move on.*
To write with a clear, personal voice	Your own 'take' on the question is made obvious to the examiner. You are not just repeating other people's ideas, but offering what **you** think.	Although you may mention different perspectives on the task, you settle on your own view. Use language that shows careful, but confident, consideration. For example: *I think that it is only by laughing at the characters that we come to care about what happens to them and are interested in debating what happens after the fall of the curtain.*
Construct a coherent argument	The examiner or marker can follow your train of thought so that your own viewpoint is clear to him or her.	Write in clear paragraphs that deal logically with different aspects of the question. Support what you say with well-selected and relevant evidence. Use a range of connectives to help 'signpost' your argument. For example: *We might say that Nora and Helmer are comic caricatures in their conformity to stereotype. However, when they are performing these to the point of absurdity Ibsen allows them to comment on one another – Helmer snaps 'Don't be so melodramatic', and Nora describes her disillusion when he fails to produce the 'miracle' she expected. Moreover, Ibsen is careful to show moments of real affection between them. The comedy is not simplistic, but varied, to make us think.*

Answering a 'viewpoint' question

Let us look at another question:

> 'Emotional intensity is generated not simply by the feelings expressed in a text but by the struggles of the characters to voice them.'
>
> To what extent do you agree with this view in relation to the two texts you have studied, bearing in mind the ways the writers have constructed their texts?

Stage 1: Decode the question

Underline/highlight the **key words**, and make sure you understand what the statement, quotation or viewpoint is saying. In this case:

'**To what extent do you agree …**' means: *Do you wholly agree with this statement or are there aspects of it that you would dispute?*

'**Emotional intensity …**' means: *the impact achieved by the most powerful moments in the text*

'**struggles to voice'** … means: *that you need to examine this aspect of the characters across the arc of the whole text*

So you are being asked whether you agree/disagree with the view that Ibsen's play depends for its impact on Nora's struggle towards finding a voice.

Stage 2: Decide what your viewpoint is

Examiners have stated that they tend to reward a strong view which is clearly put. Disagreeing strongly can lead to higher marks, provided you have **genuine evidence** to support your point of view. However, don't disagree just for the sake of it.

Stage 3: Decide how to structure your answer

Pick out the key points you wish to make, and decide on the order that you will present them in. Keep this basic plan to hand while you write your response.

Stage 4: Write your response

Begin by expanding on the aspect or topic mentioned in the task title. In this way, you can set up the key ideas you will explore. For example:

The most famous moment in 'A Doll's House' is the slamming of the door as Nora leaves Helmer. It is no coincidence that Ibsen chose an action, involving a powerful sound effect, rather than a speech, to conclude the story. Nora has found the words to say what she needs, but words are not enough to make the point by themselves.

Then in the remaining paragraphs proceed to set out the different arguments or perspectives, including your own.

In the final paragraph, end with a clear statement of your viewpoint, but do not list or go over the points you have made. End succinctly and concisely.

Then, proceed to dealing with the second text in a similar way.

EXAMINER'S TIP

You should comment concisely, professionally and thoughtfully and present a range of viewpoints. Try using modal verbs such as 'would', 'could', 'might', 'may' to clarify your own interpretation. For example, *I would argue that Nora's struggles towards articulacy begin from the very outset, with the word 'Hide'. She is certainly ignorant about 'society', but there always seems to be something she feels forbidden to say; this may be related to the way she finds it easier to lie to Helmer than to conduct a rational argument.*

COMPARING *A DOLL'S HOUSE* WITH OTHER TEXTS

As part of your assessment, you may have to compare *A Doll's House* with – or link it to – other texts you have studied. These may be novels or poetry. You may also have to link or draw in references from texts written by critics.

Linking or comparison questions might relate specifically to the genre of political and social protest writing. For example:

> **Political and social protest writing often focuses on relationships between the powerful and the powerless. Explore the significance of such a relationship in two political and social protest texts you have studied.**

Or, more generally about a key aspect of the text:

> **'Men may seem to be more powerful than women, but the reality is very different.' In the light of this, consider ways in which writers explore power and gender. In your answer, compare one drama text and one poetry text from the above lists. By comparing *A Doll's House* with at least one other text prescribed for this topic, discuss how far you agree with this view.**

You will need to:

Evaluate the issue or statement and have an **open-minded approach**. The best answers suggest meaning**s** and interpretation**s** (plural):

- For example, in relation to the first question: do you agree that this is a feature of protest writing? Is this aspect more important in one text than in another? Why? How?
- What are the different ways in which this question or aspect can be read or viewed?
- What evidence is there in each text for this? How can you present it in a thoughtful, reflective way?
- What are the points of similarity and difference?

Express **original or creative approaches** fluently:

- This isn't about coming up with entirely new ideas, but you need to show that you're actively engaged with thinking about the question, not just reeling off things you have learnt.
- **Synthesise** your ideas – pull ideas and points together to create something fresh.
- This is a linking/comparison response, so ensure that you guide your reader through your ideas logically, clearly and with professional language.

Know ***what* to compare/contrast**: the writer's methods – **form, structure** and **language** – will **always** be central to your response. Consider:

- The authorial perspective or voice (who is speaking/writing) in verse or prose narrative: the variety of perspectives in drama, provided by different characters or by the relationship between words and action; the visual stage picture; the way the flow of time is managed in different texts.
- Different characteristic use of language (language, dialect, imagery, varied voices, the difference between the exploration of an idea on stage and in a novel or poem)
- Variety of symbols, images, motifs, stage images, stage directions, movement (how they represent concerns of the author/time; what they are and how and where they appear; how they link to critical perspectives; their purposes, effects and impact on the reader and/or audience.
- Shared or differing approaches (to what extent do Ibsen and the author(s) of Text 2/3 conform to/challenge/subvert approaches to writing about social protest and change?)

Writing your response

'Emotional intensity is generated not simply by the feelings expressed in a text but by the struggles of the characters to voice them.'

To what extent do you agree with this view in relation to the two texts you have studied, bearing in mind the ways the writers have constructed their texts?

Introduction to your response

- Either discuss quickly what 'emotional intensity' and 'struggle to voice' mean, and how well this applies to *A Doll's House* and the other text you have studied, or start with a particular moment from one of the texts which allows you to launch your exploration. For example:

'Does it occur to you that this is the first time we two, you and I, man and wife, have ever had a serious talk together?' Nora and Helmer have been together eight years. In that time she has not been silent. Rather, she has become a woman of many voices, none of them fully her own. She is fluent in the kind of baby-talk about 'skylarks' and 'squirrels' she uses when she needs money from Helmer. She is a competent liar, smoothly deflecting questions about forbidden sweets. She has also learnt the language of business, as she tells Mrs Linde, but uses it only in secret.

Main body of your response

- **Point 1**: continue your exploration of the struggle for articulacy in *A Doll's House*: what it implies about society; how Ibsen fitted it to the issues of the time; why this was/was not 'interesting' for readers and audiences at the time, and readers now. How might we interpret that relationship differently through time?
- **Point 2**: now cover a new factor or aspect through comparison or contrast of this relationship with another in Text 2. For example, *Tony Harrison, in 'V', shows a character expressing himself through spraying crude words on a tombstone.* How is the question of articulacy in Text 2 presented **differently or similarly** by the writer according to language, form, structures used; why was this done in this way?
- **Points 3, 4, 5, etc.**: address a range of other factors and aspects, for example other aspects of the struggle for articulacy **either** within *A Doll's House* **or** in both *A Doll's House* and the other text. What different ways do you respond to these (with more empathy, greater criticism, less interest) – and why? For example:

Ibsen prepares carefully for Nora's speech in Act Three, where she is finally able to tell Helmer – and indeed herself – how she has been silent for so long. He presents a series of incidents which change the smooth progress of life in the Helmer household. The arrival of Nora's old friend, now a woman of business, allows her to speak of work to someone who understands. Dr Rank's admission of love confronts her with a choice: she can behave to him as she does to Helmer, wheedling money by manipulating his affection, or she can face the essentially shabby nature of such behaviour. Krogstad is the first person to jolt her melodramatic sensibilities with his graphic image of suicide. All theses incidents change Nora and her language.

EXAMINER'S TIP

Remember that in order to score highly in your answer you will also need to discuss what the critics say (AO5) and consider relevant cultural or contextual factors (AO3).

Conclusion

- Synthesise elements of what you have said into a succinct final paragraph which leaves the marker with the sense that you have engaged with this task and the texts. For example:

In 'V', articulacy remains primarily the possession of the privileged poet. Although he provokes the sprayer into angry fluency their dialogue does not achieve anything new; he has to accept that and make the best of it, telling visitors to his grave to clean the obscenities but leave one small v. In 'A Doll's House', however, voice is precious; we have seen Nora grow out of all recognition, heard Krogstad speak of happiness because Mrs Linde has a voice to claim him. Even Helmer, perhaps, may stop relying on the words of church and state, and speak for himself.

USING CRITICAL INTERPRETATIONS AND PERSPECTIVES

What is a critical interpretation?

The particular way a text is viewed or understood can be called an interpretation, and can be made by literary critics (specialists in studying literary texts), reviewers, or everyday readers and students. It is about taking a position on particular elements of the text, or on what others say about it. For example you could consider:

1. Notions of 'character'

What **sort/type** of person Nora – or another character – is:

● Is she an 'archetype' (a specific type of character with common features)? For instance, she has something in common with the figure of the *ingénue* of stock companies of the time, a pretty and innocent young girl – although Ibsen gradually subverts this notion.

● Does she personify, symbolise or represent a specific idea ('The New Woman')?

● Is she modern, universal, of her time, historically accurate, etc.? (Some modern productions reproduce the period as accurately as possible to show her as a product of her environment, while others adapt the play to local, contemporary conditions.)

2. Ideas and issues

What the play tells us about **certain ideas or issues** and how we interpret them. For example:

● How society is structured: the world of the play is dominated by money and debt. Krogstad and Nora both find themselves ostracised when their crimes – forging documents to obtain money for their families – are discovered. Helmer has a secure position and a good salary, but he is in constant fear of debt and terrified that his reputation at the bank will suffer if he does not conform to the expected image.

● The role of men/women: throughout the nineteenth century there was growing agitation for women's suffrage; women had begun to demand, and secure, the right to further education, to hold positions of responsibility, and to be allowed to divorce. Nora's personal life begins to change as these new possibilities impact on her.

● Moral codes and social justice: criminal, or at least morally dubious, behaviour plays a significant role in the play. Darwin's ideas about heredity made people wonder whether morality itself was inherited. Characters in the play have different views on this subject.

3. Links and contexts

To what extent the play **links with, follows or pre-echoes** other texts and/or ideas. For example:

● George Bernard Shaw wrote *Candida* in 1894 as a response to *A Doll's House;* unlike Nora, his heroine chooses to stay with her husband. While Nora cannot forgive her disillusion with Helmer's failure to be a hero, Candida decides to stay because she sees the weakness behind the heroic exterior of her Christian Socialist spouse.

● Caryl Churchill's 1979 play *Cloud Nine* plays with time and creates surreal images to explore Victorian gender relations. The downtrodden wife Betty is played by a man – because, like Nora, she is 'a man's creation'; her daughter is portrayed by a doll. Only in the twentieth century are their roles acted by women.

● Ibsen's next play, *Ghosts* (1881), asked what would happen if a wife stayed, instead of walking out of an unsatisfactory marriage.

EXAMINER'S TIP

Make sure you have thoroughly explored the different types of criticism written about *A Doll's House*. Bear in mind that views of texts can change over time as values and experiences themselves change, and that criticism can be written for different purposes.

---

4. Genre and dramatic methods

How the play relates to **dramatic genres** and how Ibsen **constructs** the drama:

- Does it follow particular dramatic conventions, for example of the 'well-made' format?
- What are the functions of specific events, characters, plot devices, locations, etc. in relation to dramatic methods or genre?
- What are the specific moments of tension, conflict, crisis and dénouement – and do we agree on what they are?

5. Audience and critical reaction

How the play **works on an audience or reader**, and whether this changes over time and in different contexts:

- How does Ibsen **position** the audience? Are we to empathise with, feel distance from, judge and/or evaluate the events and characters?
- How do different readers view the play? For example, different critics over time, or different audiences in the 1890s, postmodern and more recent years.

Writing about critical perspectives

The important thing to remember is that **you** are a critic too. Your job is to evaluate what a critic or school of criticism has said about the elements above, arrive at your own conclusions, and also express your own ideas.

In essence, you need to: **consider** the views of others, **synthesise** them, then decide on **your perspective**.

Explain the viewpoints

Critical view A about self-determination:

> *A Marxist critic might explore images such as the weary maid in her night-clothes having Krogstad's letter roughly snatched from her – to show how social relations are primarily determined by money. As a well-fed bourgeois woman with some clerical job prospects, Nora has the luxury of making choices.*

Critical view B about the same aspect:

> *A gendered reading might suggest that all the characters are performing gender stereotypes which inevitably construct all exchanges between the sexes as power relationships.*

Then synthesise and add your perspective

> *Both readings focus on the way characters in 'A Doll's House' are inhibited from making decisions that define them. Helmer's ethics are determined by what he thinks the bank might approve of; Nora's behaviour is shaped by the ideals of womanliness promoted by her husband and father. At the end, Ibsen allows his central female character to decide that she must discover her own moral code by asking questions. The play is full of questions: about heredity, about morality, about love and marriage. I think we are shown a group of characters groping towards defining themselves even in very adverse circumstances. The nurse has learnt to love Nora; Krogstad and Mrs Linde choose to become a couple. Whether Nora can transcend all the roles imposed on her is not yet clear; whether Helmer has even begun to grasp the need to do so is also uncertain. The dynamic, open quality of the ending is what, for me, makes the play so powerful.*

 KEY INTERPRETATION

Here are just two examples of different kinds of response to *A Doll's House*:

Critic 1 – Ronald Gray considers that Ibsen fails to show the delicacy of later naturalistic writers and depends heavily on devices like compromising letters or the 'strong curtain' that concludes each act, rather than illuminating the character of Nora.

Critic 2 – Mick Wallis and Simon Shepherd consider that Ibsen is showing Nora as living her life *as if* it were a melodrama, and learning painfully that people are not theatrical 'types' – Helmer is not a noble hero, Krogstad has complex motivation for his actions.

ANNOTATED SAMPLE ANSWERS

Below are extracts from three sample answers at different levels to the same AQA/B style task/question. Bear in mind that these responses may not correspond exactly to the style of question you might face, but they will give a broad indication of some of the key skills required.

> 'As the play ends, it is clear that Nora has lost much more than she has gained.' To what extent do you agree with this view? Remember to include in your answer relevant detailed exploration of Ibsen's dramatic methods.

Candidate 1

A01 | Solid grasp of text

At the end of the play Nora leaves her husband and children. I think she does not really know what she is doing as she says she does 'not know what will happen' to her and her plans are a bit vague – she is going to her home town, but her parents are dead so there is nobody there for her. She is just angry and upset that Helmer did not do the 'miracle' she wanted and is going on an impulse. I think it was very foolish to expect the 'miracle'. Why should Helmer take the blame for something she has done? It is not fair of her to leave him for this reason and it is typical of her selfish thinking. Nora always thinks of every situation in terms of how it affects her, like when Dr Rank is going to tell her something and she thinks he is going to talk about her and Krogstad and is 'relieved' when he says he is dying.

A01 | Some personal interpretation, though it tends to be geared towards characterisation rather than addressing the question

A03 | Attempt to put in context – basic but useful information

By the end of the play Nora has nobody. Mrs Linde has now got Krogstad and his family to care about, and she deserves it because she has worked hard and travelled miles to find him again. I think that Ibsen put Mrs Linde in the play as an image of what a woman could gain from all the changes that were taking place in the nineteenth century. Mrs Linde travels, and has a job and is independent. So it is not that Ibsen thought women should know their place, or that they will lose too much if they try to cope on their own. Mrs Linde is like an alternative Nora. But Ibsen has chosen to make his central character a selfish heroine who loses everything through her own fault.

A02 | An interesting point, but needs development

A02 | Both quotations are very brief but they cover the point well

Helmer says that he 'has the strength to change'. This may well be true, he really loves Nora. He likes giving her presents and she says that he has always been 'kind' to her, so we should take this idea seriously. Nora does not really give him a chance. She says that she does not love him any more, but what she really means is that she will not forgive him for the one time he says something selfish, about how he is 'saved'. Helmer is willing to forgive Nora for going to Krogstad. This shows that she is throwing away the relationship without trying, while Helmer is willing to try.

Nora loses her children as well. We know that she loves them and we see that she sees a lot of them normally. She refuses to see them in the last scene, and I think it is because it would be too painful. She is not really thinking the situation through. We get an idea about what she is losing though, because Ibsen has put the nurse in the play.

A04 Might be a useful point to connect with other texts

The nurse had to give up her baby and did not have any choice because society was very hard on unmarried mothers.

Nora asks her about it, so she knows that not everybody is as lucky as she is. The nurse loves Nora and does not say how much it hurt to lose her baby because that would hurt Nora, but the audience understands. Nora says that the children are 'in better hands than mine', by which she means the nurse, and she is right to trust her, but does not think about the pain it will cause.

A05 Aware of the pros and cons – could develop this by quoting some specific critical views

Nora does gain her independence. She says that she can get work and we know that she has managed to work and save in the past. But she has not always been very intelligent. She should have known that the forged signature was a silly idea and that she would get found out. She says that she has been brought up by her father to be like a little doll and this is probably true, but she has not learnt very much yet.

A02 Attempt to get to grips with language – worth developing this point further

When she talks to Mrs Linde about earning money it is in a very childish way, about 'things called quarterly instalments', so she may not actually be as fit to work as she thinks she is. Krogstad has to explain a lot of things to her about the law that seem very obvious, like forging a signature being a crime. Nora does tell a lot of lies – like about the macaroons – which is also childish. She does not really face up to the truth of things. Some of this is to protect Helmer, like about the holiday, but it seems to be her instinct to dodge any difficult confrontations. She would rather get the money out of Rank than tell Helmer the truth, and when this does not work the only answer she can think of is killing herself. I think Nora may not be ready for the world yet and is going to regret leaving.

MID LEVEL

Comment

- A clear and methodical approach, consistently weighing up pros and cons in a basic but consistent way. Needs to push the analysis further to move it beyond broad observations, but fundamentals of critical reading are in place.
- Broad sense of ways in which meaning is shaped in *A Doll's House*. Closer attention to language and technique would have raised the level of the analysis.
- Makes reference to historical context but critical engagement with it needs further development.
- No connections with other texts in this part of the question.
- This answer is marked by basic yet consistent critical evaluation, which demonstrates awareness of point of view. Doesn't engage with more sophisticated critical perspectives.

To improve the answer:

- Pay closer attention to the way meaning may be shaped by use of language and literary techniques. (AO2)
- Engage more purposefully with relevant historical and literary contexts. (AO3/AO4)
- Develop a more sophisticated understanding of how critical interpretations might shed light on key issues. (AO5)

Candidate 2

A01 Good opening with apt quotation

'I've been living here like a pauper, from hand to mouth.' I think Nora is right. She has nothing, and therefore has nothing to lose at the end of the play. Helmer of course finds this very difficult to grasp, as he sees himself as a generous husband; but throughout the play we see Nora in situations where she finds herself lacking what she needs – sometimes in material terms, sometimes in political or spiritual ones.

We soon learn that not only does Nora have to ask, as a pauper must, for money to feed and clothe the family, but that she cannot have it without pleasing Helmer by doing 'tricks' – literally dancing for him 'in the moonlight'. While Helmer is not ungenerous and seems to enjoy giving her 'something in gold paper', Nora has no financial security to speak of. The debt to Krogstad has made this situation worse. Her clothes, the presents she buys for others, in fact everything that is not for Helmer or the things the children really need, cost very little; but she has to pretend that they are expensive in order to keep some money back for the debt. Hence everything she owns seems to have a lie linked to it. Even the macaroons are forbidden, and she has to hide them. Although Ibsen uses them for comic effect, they also stress that she is, as she says, living 'from hand to mouth'. In my view Nora is as penniless at the beginning of the play as she is at the end – but at the end, she is the one who chooses to be so, which is arguably a slight gain.

A01 Develops point

A02 Good point which could be developed to explore Ibsen's complex symbolism here

Early critics were so disturbed by Nora abandoning her children at the end of the play that they tended to say it was psychologically impossible – Brun described it as 'screaming dissonance'. While most people can at least accept that some women, not necessarily monsters, do behave in this way, the children can surely be seen as Nora's greatest 'loss'. I think Ibsen intended his audience to debate this. This is not a 'happy ending'.

A05 A good point to consider implications of naturalism

A05 Useful reference to early critical view, but relate also to some later critical views

A02 Useful point, but needs to be more tightly related to the next paragraph – show how this is structured to make that debate happen

However, for much of the play, Nora has been thinking of herself as a bad mother. When Helmer talks about 'mothers who are constitutional liars' he may not even mean what he is saying – he likes to make speeches – but Nora takes it completely to heart. After the happy games we see in the first act we might expect to see Nora in her element at Christmas, with even the strain of the debt alleviated by the happiness of being with the children. Instead she avoids them, and there is nobody to advise her; the nurse accepts her decision and says that they 'can get used to anything'. Nora may be applying that to herself, as well as the children, as she goes on to question the nurse about how such a loss might feel. It is, clearly, going to cause her pain to leave the children, but Helmer's words have struck so deep that she has already given up a large element of her motherhood. In a way it is Helmer who has already deprived her. Later he threatens to take them away from her;

A02 Useful point – develop the question of audience expectation

Nora thinks that he is right, even if he says it for all the wrong reasons. She does not give up the children lightly – but she is clear that she, and they, might both be the losers if she stays.

> **AO3** Good point but worth exploring with reference to the legal situation at the time – Nora has no rights

Nora also loses Helmer. His pomposity, his intolerance and his steady refusal to think of Nora as an adult – even when her attitude is clearly more mature than his own, as in the final conversation with Dr Rank – might lead some to argue that he is not much of a loss. Others might point to remarks like 'You've always been so kind,' and to their more playful moments, when they both seem to find it fun that she is his 'skylark'. However, I think that the problem is deeper than this. Although she and Helmer have both found some pleasure and contentment in their marriage, it seems that Nora has never really chosen her husband for herself. Helmer has been 'kind and helpful' to her father, who has been in some financial or legal trouble. Nora seems to have been a reward for his trouble. Her analysis is that she 'passed from papa's hands into yours'. (Helmer confirms this view of events when he complains that he is being punished for this by Krogstad, and that Nora is as dishonest as her father.) Nora cannot really be said to have had a marriage, in the sense of a freely chosen partnership.

> **AO2** Well balanced paragraph with clear conclusion

> **AO3** Needs to develop context here – a good point, but introduced rather late

Thus, when Nora walks out into the darkness, she has gained more than she has lost. While she is leaving her family, they have never fully belonged to her; she has no money, but she knows that she can earn that. Nora was a heroine for the early feminist movement. I think she is also a heroine to herself, and that this is a real gain.

GOOD LEVEL

Comment

- A pleasingly personal, if slightly loose, response.
- Careful attention to structure and to the way the text explores different viewpoints.
- Touches on context, although this needs development.
- Some critical views are cited, but needs a stronger critical framework.

To improve the answer:

- Tighten the argument so that it appears a thought-out and well-directed answer rather than a series of useful and more loosely related insights. (AO1)
- Make more focused reference to historical and literary contexts. (AO3/AO4)
- Sharpen the sense of how a critical perspective shapes the interpretation of a text. (AO5)

Candidate 3

A01 Useful and relevant source material and a striking opening

'My Nora went alone.' Ibsen said this to a woman who left her husband for a lover and who claimed to identify herself with his heroine. Nora walks into the darkness of a winter night. She has no protector, no children, and no money (even though Helmer offers some). It was important to Ibsen that Nora did not 'gain' materially by leaving; he made it clear to the audience that her choice involved sacrifice, but left them to debate whether she had, or had not, gained anything else.

The audience may have been shocked at the idea of a woman abandoning a comfortable home, security and a regular income, at a time when most women had to marry to obtain them. As a modern spectator, however, I cannot see these 'losses' as disastrous. Nora has proved herself capable of earning money as a copyist, as intelligent and resourceful as Mrs Linde, the embodiment of the independent female nineteenth-century feminists called the New Woman.

A03 Historical context linked to text

A02 Good awareness of the way the plot is developed

However, Nora loses Helmer and the children – a far more serious loss. Although she is profoundly disillusioned with the man from whom she expected a 'miracle', there is a bond between them. Ibsen initially stresses their playfulness, suggesting they can be happy together; Nora begins to resent her childlike 'skylark' persona only when under pressure to hide her true situation. She evidently finds Helmer attractive, telling him that living together as brother and sister would 'not last'. In David Thacker's 1992 production for the BBC, Trevor Eve and Juliet Stevenson played the parting in tears, showing the cost to both.

A05 Relevant interpretation, which will link to later point about different readings

A01 Good textual knowledge extending to alternative version

The children are an even greater loss. Directors at the time forced Ibsen to write an ending in which Nora stays. However, in his alternative version he makes Nora 'collapse' after this decision – a graphic image of the psychological price of staying.

Nora is a loving mother, as we see in her interaction with her children in Act One. But Helmer's conviction that lying parents are 'poison' leads her to withdraw from them. To some extent, then, she has – unwillingly – 'lost' the children before Christmas Day. Later, Helmer decides to deny her any contact with them. This is a threat born of temporary rage – but it is important to realise he would be within his rights. Even the most indulgent nineteenth-century husband took for granted his right to decide his children's education, religious upbringing and lifestyle without reference to his wife. Helmer's anger vividly brings home the limits of a mother's power to Nora (and us). Though her loss is terrible, she may be right to say that she 'can be nothing' to her children unless the relationship changes drastically.

A02 Awareness of importance of stage directions

A03 Links context to the text

I think it is incorrect to say that Nora has lost more than she has gained, because in her aloneness she has found the beginnings of a self. From his opening words, 'Is that my skylark?', it is plain that Helmer has imposed upon her the image of what patriarchy wants her

A01 A clear and well-articulated personal response

to be: pretty, obedient and ignorant. The only real decision she has ever made is to borrow the money. Despite the strain this causes, she takes pride in her new identity as working woman – but the secrecy involved suggests that she can only make life-defining decisions away from Helmer, outside the home. She can only define herself once she leaves. As yet, she is not a fully-realised person, but a male construct of femininity – as she rightly says, a 'doll', for her father and Helmer to play with and dress to their taste. Nobody could be expected to see existential nullity as a fair price to pay for family love.

A02 Usefully explores how symbolism shapes audience response

I cannot agree with the assumption underlying this question – that the final curtain is the last word. Ibsen is not tying up loose ends in the way satirised by Wilde in 'The Importance of Being Earnest' – 'The good ended happily, the bad unhappily. That is what fiction means.' He gives his plot the untidiness and ambiguity of real life, which actors can explore in different ways. The ending is the beginning of a new story. As Nora says, 'I've no idea what will happen to me.' She walks into the dark – but throughout the play she has been linked (especially by Rank) to light and optimism. It is for the reader, or the actor, to imagine what happens next and whether their particular Nora loses or gains.

A04 Useful connection which illuminates Ibsen's naturalism

A01 Carefully structured conclusion which integrates critical viewpoint with its own understanding of the question

Some critics have suggested that the ending is contrived – a 'strong curtain'. Robert Ferguson points out that 'Nora has already proved herself the stronger', and considers the parting psychologically unnecessary for Nora or Helmer. However, Nora says that Helmer can only change if his 'doll' is taken away from him. I think that she is right. I would choose to play Nora here as perceptive, not unkind. She has to risk losing Helmer for ever, because although his broken sentences show his pain, he tries to keep Nora by appealing to various authorities – the Church, the Law – rather than thinking for himself. He does not yet have a voice of his own to say that he loves and wants her. Toril Moi says that Nora 'demands nothing short of a revolutionary consideration of the very meaning of love.' This is a great deal to ask – but the play does not exclude the possibility of the 'miracle of miracles'. Nora is still forging a self; Helmer at least knows that he must do so if he is to win Nora – and she him. They may yet become a truly modern couple. The Nora walking into a new day may gain not just a self, but everything else as well.

A02 Awareness of multiple possibilities in the text, and ability to make a clear personal choice in support of argument

VERY HIGH LEVEL

Comment

- An impressively coherent and creative personal response. In control of materials and of the construction of a persuasive argument.
- Use of quotations has a confidence that reflects an assured grasp of ways in which meaning is shaped in the text.
- Focused and refreshing engagement with historical context.
- Secondary literary and critical materials used with precision and purpose.
- Astute and assured reference to critical approaches and the light they might shed on central issues of the text.

PRACTICE TASK

Now it's your turn to work through an AQA/B exam-style task on *A Doll's House*. The key is to:

- Quickly read and decode the task/question
- Briefly plan your points – then add a few more details, such as evidence, or make links between them
- Write your answer

Decode the question

> **'Political and social protest writing often focuses on rebellion against those in power.'**
>
> **Explore the significance of rebellion as it is presented in two political and social protest texts you have studied.**

EXAMINER'S TIP

Remember to incorportate the views of critics, but make sure that the central idea is your own!

'Political and social …. rebellion'	suggests that a common element in political and social protest writing is 'rebellion'
'rebellion'	can mean 'political resistance' but here could also mean 'personal struggle' (given that in many cases – especially for feminists – the personal is political)
'To what extent do you agree?'	What is my view? Do I agree with the statement completely, partially or not at all?
'focuses'	What has Ibsen done that supports (or doesn't support) this idea?

Plan and write

- Decide your viewpoint
- Plan your points
- Think of key evidence and quotations
- Write your answer

Success criteria

- Show your understanding of political and social protest writing as a genre
- Draw on a range of critical views or different interpretation as appropriate
- Sustain your focus on the idea of 'rebellion'
- Make links and connections between the two texts
- Argue your point of view clearly and logically
- Make perceptive points and express your ideas confidently
- Support your points with relevant, well-chosen evidence including quotations
- Use literary terminology accurately and appropriately with reference to the effect on the reader
- Write in fluent, controlled and accurate English

Once you have finished, use the **Mark scheme** on page 120 to evaluate your response.

FURTHER READING

The text and other plays by Ibsen

A Doll's House, translated by Michael Meyer, Bloomsbury Methuen Drama, 2016
  This is the edition of the text used in the preparation of these Notes

Plays: One, trans. Michael Meyer, Methuen, 1980
  Includes *Ghosts*, in which a wife stays in a troubled marriage

Plays: Two, trans. Michael Meyer, Methuen, 1980
  Includes *Hedda Gabler,* which develops the theme of marriage

Six Plays by Henrik Ibsen, trans. Eva Le Gallienne, Modern Library, 1951
  Includes Le Gallienne's translation of *A Doll's House,* omitting the silk stockings scene

Criticism

Harold Clurman, *Ibsen*, Macmillan, 1977
  A director's view of some of the major plays, with some useful theatrical insights

Michael Egan, *Ibsen: The Critical Heritage*, Routledge & Kegan Paul, 1972
  Reviews from the first British productions

Ronald Gray, *Ibsen: A Dissenting View*, Cambridge University Press, 1977
  Sums up the main arguments against Ibsen since the 1950s

Frode Helland, *Ibsen in Practice,* Bloomsbury 2015
  Studies of worldwide productions and analysis of their significance

James McFarlane, ed., *The Cambridge Companion to Ibsen*, Cambridge University Press, 1994
  Collection of essays with a useful general introduction and detailed bibliography

Michael Mangan, *Staging Masculinities: History, Gender, Performance*, Palgrave, 2002
  Discusses the construction of masculinity in the theatre and explores *A Doll's House* in detail

Frederick J. Marker and Lise-Lone Marker, *Ibsen's Lively Art: A Performance Study of the Major Plays*, Cambridge University Press, 1989
  Explores Ibsen in the theatre and discusses contrasting versions of *A Doll's House*

Toril Moi, *Henrik Ibsen and the Birth of Modernism: Art, Theater, Philosophy*, OUP, 2006
  Innovative study which reappraises Ibsen's role in literary history

Elizabeth Robins, *Ibsen and the Actress*, reprinted Haskell House, 1973
  Pamphlet describing the impact of Ibsen on her artistic and political life

George Bernard Shaw, *The Quintessence of Ibsenism*, Constable and Company, 1932
  Originally written for a Fabian Society meeting in 1890

Alisa Solomon, *Re-Dressing the Canon,* Routledge, 1997
  Important essay on criticism and gender in *A Doll's House*

Joan Templeton, *Ibsen's Women*, Cambridge University Press, 2001
  Explores the influence of women on Ibsen; a feminist reading of *A Doll's House*

Raymond Williams, *Drama from Ibsen to Brecht*, Pelican, 1976
  Most influential study of the later twentieth century

On naturalism and playmaking

William Archer, *Play-Making*, reprinted Dodo Press, 2006

David Edgar, *How Plays Work*, Nick Hern Books, 2009

Konstantin Stanislavsky, *An Actor Prepares*, trans. Elizabeth Hapgood, Methuen, 1979

Lee Strasberg, *A Dream of Passion: The Development of the Method*, Bloomsbury, 1988

J. L. Styan, *Modern Drama in Theory and Practice: Realism and Naturalism*, Cambridge University Press, 1981

John Russell Taylor, *The Rise and Fall of the Well Made Play*, Methuen, 1967
  Discusses the development of the **well-made play** both before and after the impact of Ibsen.

Mick Wallis and Simon Shepherd, *Studying Plays*, Arnold, 1998
  Excellent introduction to theatre studies

Biography

Robert Ferguson, *Henrik Ibsen: A New Biography*, Richard Cohen Books, 1996
  Most up-to-date life of Ibsen, describing his development as a writer through working in the theatre

General

Judith Butler, *Gender Trouble: Feminism and the Subversion of Identity*, Routledge, 1990
  A difficult but rewarding study of how people perform their gender

Terry Eagleton, *Literary Theory: An Introduction*, Blackwell, 1996
  Clear discussion of major literary theories

Some linked texts

Geoffrey Chaucer, *The Merchant's Prologue and Tale,* CUP, 2002

Charles Dickens, *David Copperfield*

Tony Harrison, *V,* in *Selected Poems,* Penguin, 1987

Arthur Miller, *All My Sons,* Penguin Modern Classics, 2015

Friedrich Schiller, *Don Carlos,* World's Classics, 2002

George Bernard Shaw, *Plays Pleasant* and *Plays Unpleasant,* Penguin, 2003

LITERARY TERMS

body language how people show their feelings by the way they move, sit or stand – often revealing that these are different from those which they are expressing in words.

cliché a widely used expression which has lost impact through overuse.

colloquial everyday speech used by people in informal situations.

comedy a story with a happy ending, most commonly, but not exclusively, used of plays.

commodification treating someone as an object to be sold on the market.

confidant, confidante a **stock character** whose function is to listen to the confidences and intentions of the **protagonist**.

dénouement the point in the play where the whole plot has finally unfolded (from the French for 'untying a knot').

development and complication the central section of a **well-made play** which makes the situation more complex and creates **suspense** about the outcome.

double entendre a word or phrase open to two interpretations, one of which is usually slightly indecent.

double take a comic technique where the actor does not instantly react to a shock, and then suddenly realises what has occurred.

drag act a performance in the clothes of the opposite sex, such as that of a pantomime dame, traditionally played by a man.

euphemism an inoffensive word or phrase substituted for one considered offensive or hurtful.

existentialism the idea that we are shaped by the choices that we make rather than possessing innate qualities.

exposition the opening of a play in which all the information that the audience needs in order to understand the situation is put over. In a **well-made play** the playwright tries to do this without making the fact obvious.

foil character whose main function is to provide a contrast to the central figure.

fourth wall naturalistic plays these are often set in rooms; effectively, one 'wall' of these rooms is removed, allowing the audience to look in.

hegemony term coined by the Marxist philosopher Antonio Gramsci; it means that a diverse culture can be ruled or dominated by one group or class.

imagery descriptive language which uses images to make actions, objects and characters more vivid in the reader's mind. **Metaphors** and similes are examples of imagery.

ingénue term for the innocent young heroine of the play; nineteenth- and early twentieth-century companies would employ an actress who specialised in such roles.

irony incongruity between what might be expected and what actually happens; the ill-timed arrival of an event that had been hoped for; the humorous or sarcastic use of words to imply the opposite of what they normally mean.

melodrama a popular theatrical genre of the nineteenth century. Distinguished by moralistic plots – often rooted in class struggle – with sensational effects. Music played an important role; originally it was used to evade the licensing laws which made it difficult for theatres to stage spoken drama, but it became important as a device to heighten the emotion of climactic moments.

metaphor a figure of speech in which a word or phrase is applied to an object, a character or an action which does not literally belong to it, in order to imply a resemblance and create an unusual or striking image in the reader's mind.

metatheatre a term used to describe drama about drama; metatheatrical plays openly draw attention to their theatricality by the use of such devices as asides and **soliloquies**, role playing and songs. Plays within plays are also implicitly metatheatrical.

modernism cultural shift during the decades just before and after the First World War. Modernists rejected traditional forms of art and literature in order to confront the new social and political aspects of an industrialised world in which values were changing.

motivation the desires and intentions that drive characters in **naturalistic** drama to behave as they do.

naturalistic, naturalism theatrical style which tries to create the illusion of reality on the stage. The actors do not address the audience, but behave as if they are unaware of them; the language and situations are intended to be credible and **realistic**; and the settings mirror the real world as closely as possible.

paradox apparently contradictory statement or situation which proves to be true or viable.

patriarchy a society where the authority and ideas of men dominate over those of women.

practical term for **properties** and items of stage furniture which actually fulfil their function, as opposed to painted images.

properties, props objects used in the play, some of which may be important to the action, such as Krogstad's letter.

proscenium arch frame around the stage in theatres built during the nineteenth and early twentieth centuries. It marks the edge of the **fourth wall**.

protagonist the central character whose actions form the focus of the play.

raisonneur a detached observer who comments on the action – generally a professional man, often a doctor, like Rank.

realism literary portrayal of the 'real' world, in both physical and psychological detail, rather than an imaginary or ideal one. Nineteenth-century novels often described themselves in this way.

reification Marxist term meaning the making of human beings into commodities.

resolution final moments of a play in which the loose ends are tied up.

rhetoric structured and patterned language used in formal speech-making.

scenario a detailed plan for a play.

scène à faire term invented by French pioneers of the **well-made play** to indicate a crucial scene, usually a confrontation, which the audience would anticipate with excitement.

soliloquy a dramatic device which allows a character alone on the stage to speak directly to the audience as if thinking aloud, revealing their inner thoughts, feelings and intentions.

stage business non-verbal action on the stage, prescribed in the stage directions or added by an actor or the director.

stock character the kind of character one could expect to see in a particular genre, for example: the oppressed mother in a **melodrama**; the 'best friend' who listens to the confidences of the hero or heroine in a romantic **comedy**; the gossipy old woman who exists mainly to relay information to the audience in a **naturalistic** play.

strong curtain a powerful line of dialogue or situation which occurs just before the fall of the curtain. Generally placed immediately before the last act of the play to maximise **suspense** about the outcome.

subtext theatrical term to describe a pattern of emotions and energies that are not directly spoken about but show themselves through trivial actions or remarks which seem casual on the surface. It is a feature of **naturalistic** drama and Oscar Wilde was a pioneer of the technique in England.

suspense excitement about the outcome of the story, often raised to a high pitch just before a break in the action.

symbolic, symbolism allowing a complex idea to be represented by a single object.

tragedy in its original sense, a drama dealing with elevated actions and emotions and characters of high social standing, in which a terrible outcome becomes inevitable as a result of an unstoppable sequence of events.

well-made play the form taken by most Victorian West End drama, derived from the French dramatists Eugène Scribe and Victorien Sardou. A well-made play has a clear structure: the **exposition** tells us what we need to know (usually that some of the characters have a secret); the **development and complication** bring the situation to crisis point, usually around the end of the penultimate act, as secrets come out and throw people into confusion; finally, there is a **resolution**.

REVISION TASK ANSWERS

Revision task 1: First impressions

NORA:
- Very excited about Christmas, especially in relation to spending money – is she over-excitable?
- Husband says that she can never keep any money – perhaps she is extravagant.
- Talks childishly; does this mean she is not very clever?
- Spends in secret on macaroons – maybe selfish?

HELMER:
- The family breadwinner.
- Tries to moderate his wife's extravagance by recalling earlier problems.
- Worries about money in relation to the future, and is anxious Nora will not get into debt on the strength of his new salary before it starts.
- Perhaps rather controlling – why does Nora have to 'give her word' about not eating sweets? (p. 27) – but perhaps he needs to ensure she does not get into trouble through impulsive behaviour.

Revision task 2: Subtext

- At the start Rank is very honest, but Nora is wrapped up in her own worries. She demands that he 'laugh' (p. 65). He takes this as advice for coping with his situation.
- By joining in with Rank's new lighthearted tone and using words like 'asparagus', Nora shows that she knows but will not mention the nature of his disease, and he shows in turn that he knows her to be a sophisticated woman.
- The discussion of Mrs Linde as his 'replacement' is also lighthearted, but it expresses Rank's real feelings. Nora changes the subject – already aware he may want to speak of love?
- The 'silk stockings' conversation shows Nora flirting as a prelude to asking for money. The jokes are risqué – this shows a level of trust between them. The crudity also helps to avoid the topic of love.
- Several times Nora alludes to Helmer in a slighting way: 'I feel the same about Torvald as I did about papa' (p. 69). This remains at a lighthearted level, but suggests she would have liked to speak about the difficulties in her marriage more openly and now feels she cannot.
- The conversation around the 'lamp' can be seen as a reproach to Rank for declaring his love; lines such as 'you are a fine gentleman' (p. 69) indicate that Nora does not want him to feel too hurt, that she will pretend to treat the matter as a joke.
- The question of the loan has been avoided.

Revision task 3: Suspense

- They might assume that the next act will be set well before the 'thirty-one hours' (p. 79) are over and that Krogstad will make another move to force the issue.
- They might think that Mrs Linde will be successful in her efforts to persuade Krogstad to take back his letter – either because Krogstad really cares for her, or because as the 'villain' he might make sexual demands in return.
- They might expect Helmer to emerge as the sort of hero Nora dreams of, taking the blame on himself.
- They might wonder if Nora is really going to take her own life. They could expect a highly sentimental scene in which Helmer laments afterwards.
- They would anticipate a *scène à faire* between Helmer and Nora when he learns the truth.

Revision task 4: The final curtain

FOR:
- The audience is still thinking about the issues involved and might consider them more dispassionately without the shocking ending.
- Nora has won the battle; she does not need to punish Helmer by leaving.
- To leave young children is contrary to Nora's nature – she is not a cruel person.

AGAINST:
- The shock value is important – only through this can an audience really understand the value of a woman's freedom.
- Helmer is as yet incapable of being the sort of husband the newly-politicised Nora would want – as she says, he needs to lose his 'doll' in order to grow up.
- Nora's choice to stay is so painful to her that the play would lose its power to inspire.
- The conservatives among the audience would read her choice as 'seeing sense' rather than as the outcome of real mental struggle.
- The whole action is pervaded with the idea of parting: the death of Nora's father, the nurse's loss of her daughter, the imminent death of Rank; subconsciously, the final parting is expected.

Revision task 5: What does Nora want?

FIRST SCENE (Act One, pp. 24–8):
- Nora wants to celebrate – not simply Christmas, but her progress in paying off the debt so far.
- She wants Helmer to give her more money towards this. She may also wish that she could stop the pretence.

LAST SCENE (Act Three, pp. 92–104):
- Once the truth is known, she wants Helmer to be a hero and say that he will take the blame, the 'miracle' she expects.
- She also wants to forestall this by heroic suicide.
- When it is clear he is not a hero, she decides to leave. She wants him to understand why: 'You and I have got to face facts' (p. 97).

Revision task 6: The moral debate

- DR RANK thinks that some people are 'morally twisted' (Act One, p. 39) and are treated too leniently by society. He also puts forward the view that some people (like him) suffer unfairly for the sins of others.

- MRS LINDE thinks that 'it's the sick who need care the most' (Act One, p. 40) and that people like Krogstad deserve a second chance.
- HELMER believes lying is a source of moral corruption – he claims that he could forgive Krogstad his forgery, if he had admitted it. He thinks lies poison the home, especially those of the mother.
- NORA initially does not care about 'strangers' – she says she would not care about paying creditors if Helmer died in debt. Later, she calls Krogstad 'that poor man' and sees Helmer as 'petty' for dismissing him. (Act Two, p. 62)
- She is disturbed, and convinced, by Helmer's strictures on lying mothers, and withdraws from her children almost at once.
- She feels that she did not act wrongly in forging the signature guaranteeing the loan – she was saving her father from worry and her husband from illness.
- She finally decides that she must not take morality for granted but must 'try to find my own answer' (Act Three, p. 100).

Revision task 7: Wealth and debts

- NORA AND KROGSTAD: HE has power over Nora because she owes him money, and forged a signature to get it. SHE owes him money, but has some power over him because her husband controls his wages / employment. HE thinks that she owed him honesty in the first place. SHE owes him her reputation, and Helmer's, when he returns the paper.
- RANK AND NORA: HE has the money that would save Nora, would like to help her out of love, and feels that he owes both her and Helmer gratitude for their kindness. SHE thinks of using her power as his beloved to ask him for money, but decides that it would be immoral.
- HELMER AND NORA: HE has all the financial power as breadwinner and gives Nora money as he sees fit. SHE has to depend on him, but her secret earnings give her independence. HE feels he is owed gratitude, for helping her father, and obedience, because she is his wife. In fact he owes Nora his life.
- HELMER AND KROGSTAD: HELMER has the power to keep or dismiss Krogstad. KROGSTAD has the power to blackmail him over the forged signature. HELMER is ultimately in debt to Krogstad for returning the paper, and to Nora, to whom the paper is actually returned.

Revision task 8: Alternative curtain lines

KROGSTAD:
- Act One would have an effective curtain line with: 'If I get thrown into the gutter for a second time, I shall take you with me.' (p. 50)
- Act Two would probably conclude with Krogstad's exit: 'Goodbye, Mrs Helmer', (p. 73) but with the set arranged differently, so that we could see him putting the letter in the mailbox.
- Act Three might give Krogstad a chance to return the paper with the signature in person. He would explain his new-found happiness and be a witness to the break-up of Nora and Helmer. Might even try to comfort Helmer by telling him that everyone is capable of change.

MRS LINDE:
- Act One: She is offstage for much of this act, but would potentially be a person in whom Nora could confide her fears about being an unfit mother at the end of it.
- Act Two: She witnesses the tarantella before going into dinner. This would be a moment to focus on the revival of her feelings for Krogstad – she might reflect on what she wants from a marriage.
- Act Three: She might return with Krogstad, as they have made a mutual decision about how to act towards the Helmers. We might expect her to be proactive in helping Nora to her final exit.

Revision task 9: Nora speaks

TO HELMER: Sometimes uses the third person, talking about 'we larks and squirrels' (Act One, p. 26), as a child might. Uses his first name, Torvald, often with 'dear' added. A great deal of coaxing language – 'I'll do this if you...'; 'please'. At the end, she changes, speaking in clear, short sentences or with logical and carefully structured arguments.

TO KROGSTAD: At first rude and overbearing: 'How dare you presume ...' (Act One, p. 45). When the blackmail begins she never pleads, but her speech becomes plain: 'What do you want from me?' 'Show some heart' (Act Two, p. 71).

DR RANK: Witty and allusive, as in the discussion about asparagus, which is really about his disease; *double entendres* around the silk stockings. Her farewell uses **subtext** in a more tender way, offering 'light' (Act Three, p. 90). One of the people to whom Nora confides her urge to swear.

MRS LINDE: the only other person to whom Nora confides this. Nora's earlier speech to her is self-centred, full of 'I', 'we' and 'we're going to have heaps and heaps of money!' (Act One, p. 30) and she is childishly full of secrets, saying 'tra-la-la' (Act One, p. 35) as if they were still schoolmates. In the last act, their exchanges are very brief and to the point.

Revision task 10: A controversial play

PLAYS PLEASANT:
- Ibsen was much influenced by the comedies of Scribe and there are many comic episodes, such as the eating of the macaroons and the witty chat of Nora and Rank.
- The ending is arguably positive – Nora has grown and changed, and Helmer may do so too.
- The story of Krogstad and Mrs Linde is full of optimism and even a kind of romance.

PLAYS UNPLEASANT:
- It is a play about social change – this was certain to trouble its early audiences, even some of those well-disposed towards feminism.
- It is about the end of a loving marriage, and Helmer is broken-hearted.
- The story of Dr Rank is a tragic one.
- It shows a harsh world in which women struggle – none of them will ever be as wealthy as Helmer or Rank in their own right, and the experience of the nurse is terrible.

PROGRESS CHECK ANSWERS

Part Two: Studying *A Doll's House*

Section One: Check your understanding

1. What do we learn about Nora and Helmer from looking at their home? Make a list of key items on the stage and suggest their significance.

- There are four doors. The 'tasteful but not expensive' furnishing includes a piano, books and engravings, a stove, a small table.
- The DOORS show that it is a fairly extensive apartment and also carry a suggestion of concealment.
- The FURNISHINGS show their income level – a modest prosperity.
- The PIANO, BOOKS and ENGRAVINGS suggest they are a cultured couple, perhaps even that they have travelled abroad to acquire some of these things.
- The STOVE locates the play in Scandinavia and carries overtones of warmth.
- The TABLE will become important as a place where serious discussion takes place.

2. What things has Nora bought, and what happens to them? Make brief notes on each.

- CHRISTMAS TREE: kept from the children as a surprise; then brought on for Nora to decorate while she plans to charm Helmer into keeping Krogstad at the bank; later appears stripped of presents with the candles burnt out, reflecting Nora's despair at the start of Act Two.
- MACAROONS: Nora slyly eats these while Helmer is out of the room and hides them before he interrogates her about sweet-eating. Later she shares them with Rank and Mrs Linde, telling Dr Rank they were a gift from Mrs Linde who did not know Helmer had forbidden them. They collude in hiding them when he enters.
- TOYS: for the children at Christmas. These reflect gender roles – the boys get a sword, a trumpet and a toy horse; the girl gets a doll and a cradle.
- DRESS MATERIAL and HANDKERCHIEFS: for the maids.
- Nora has bought all these things cheaply, and feels rather guilty that the nurse at least does not have anything better.

3. What visitors come to the house, and how are they received? Write a short note on each.

- MRS LINDE: Old school friend of Nora; they confide in each other, though Nora is more voluble about her own concerns. Nora asks Helmer to take Mrs Linde on at the bank – he is happy to do so, but does not realise that he has been manipulated. He is bored by Mrs Linde and sometimes rude.

- DR RANK: Visits as he likes and has a standing invitation to dinner. Happy to see both Nora and Helmer. Nora has a warm friendship with Rank, while Helmer is secretly resentful that he calls so often.
- KROGSTAD: Visits Helmer to ask him not to dismiss him. Also visits Nora, to enlist her support by blackmailing her about the forged signature on her note of hand. Disliked by both the Helmers. He despises Helmer, but has a kind of grudging respect for Nora.

4. What differences do you notice in Nora when Helmer is not present?

- WHEN HE IS THERE: playful, childish; tells outright lies; flatters Helmer; manipulates the conversation to let him think he has chosen a topic or had an idea (like employing Mrs Linde); pretends not to be able to make decisions, even about what to wear at a party.
- WHEN HE IS NOT THERE: expresses her fears to herself; can be playful, as with Dr Rank, but at a more adult level; glad to see friends; talks about Helmer's limitations; has intimate conversations Helmer might disapprove of, e.g. with the nurse; confides secrets, such as her work, which show her as a decision-maker.

5. What games does Nora play with Helmer and why? Write a list and suggest a possible motive for each.

- She plays at being a pet animal, a 'squirrel' or a 'skylark' – this underlines her helplessness, which makes him easier to manipulate
- She dances for him 'in the moonlight' – playing on his attraction to her to get what she wants
- She persuades him to give her money 'wrapped up in pretty gold paper' on the Christmas tree – he is more generous when he thinks of himself as a generous giver rather than acknowledging that she has rights as his wife and housekeeper.

6. How many characters in the play have secrets? Make a list and suggest what might happen if each secret were discovered.

- NORA: borrowing the money, forging her father's signature on the note of hand. She thinks Helmer will be shocked, and he is, although she may not expect his decision that their marriage will continue in name only.
- KROGSTAD: his earlier dishonest dealings. Helmer dismisses him when he can no longer hide this, although he wants Krogstad to go anyway.
- DR RANK: keeps his illness generally hidden, but confides in Nora. Risk of social ostracism?
- HELMER: seems to have bent the law in the case of Nora's father. Presumably his reputation would suffer.

7. What happens to the paper with the forged signature before and during the play? Make brief notes in chronological order.

- Before the play, Nora had gone to Krogstad for a loan. He demanded a guarantor for her note of hand.
- She forged her father's signature, as she thought he was too ill to be worried with it, and gave the note to Krogstad.
- On Christmas Eve he shows it to Nora and points out that the signature and the date do not tally, and that the handwriting appears to be hers. He blackmails her into asking Helmer to let him keep his job.
- When she cannot make this happen, he writes a letter to Helmer explaining everything and puts it in the mailbox.
- When Krogstad and Mrs Linde resume their former relationship, he sends the note back to Nora.
- Helmer seizes it and destroys it.

8. How many people in the play have a soliloquy? What do they talk about? Write a short note on each.

NORA:
- End of Act One (p. 54): her fear that she may corrupt her children, a new thought.
- Act One: as she decorates the tree and thinks how she will manipulate Helmer; she speaks almost as if addressing him.
- Start of Act Two (p. 55): her fear of Krogstad – echoed again after Helmer has sent the letter of dismissal – perhaps trying to convince herself that it cannot happen
- When Krogstad leaves the letter in the box (p. 73): here, she rallies enough to ask Mrs Linde for help.
- At the end of Act Two, when she knows that Helmer will know the truth after the party: her most 'theatrical' soliloquy, but also true to her state of mind.
- Her 'goodbye' in Act Three (p. 92): as she tries to leave and is stopped by Helmer.

MRS LINDE:
- As the curtain rises on Act Three, she has a brief speech as she wonders whether Krogstad will come. This stresses her likeness to Nora, and it also emphasises to the audience that she has concerns of her own.

HELMER:
- Has a very brief soliloquy at the end of Act Three after Nora has gone; important as the first real sign of Helmer's inner life, and stresses his loneliness.

9. What do we learn about Nora's early life? Make brief notes on each event.

- Her mother died when she was young and the nurse, Anne-Marie, came to take care of her. They remain close and she trusts the nurse with her own children.
- She was at school with Mrs Linde and they remain friends.
- Her father was in trouble with the law and Helmer was 'kind and helpful'. This may have involved some less than legal activity.

- She married Helmer without any intervening period of independence.
- She was friendly with the servants at her father's house, and remains much less formal than her husband.

10. What does Nora's Neapolitan outfit mean to the characters who handle it or see her wear it? Write notes on each.

- NURSE: notes how untidy the costume is, but will not let Nora throw it out; thinks it can be mended (like the marriage?)
- NORA: increasingly hates the dress as it comes to symbolise the troubles that will happen after she has danced. However, she uses the stockings to flirt with Dr Rank as a prelude to asking for the loan, a scene which carries strong sexual overtones.
- MRS LINDE: helps Nora with the dress out of kindness. Perhaps she enjoys a little vicarious frivolity?
- DR RANK: accepts rather too readily her pretence that getting a different dress is her 'great secret' from Helmer; as a friend he should probe deeper.
- HELMER: smug that he chose it for her, unaware that it is paid for with borrowed money.

11. What do we know about the Helmers' servants? Write notes on each one.

- MAID: Helen. Announces visitors, deals with the Christmas tree, posts Helmer's letters and is summoned in the middle of the night to answer the door to receive Krogstad's final letter. Gets a useful, but not personal, gift from Nora at Christmas.
- NURSE: Anne-Marie. Became pregnant by a man who left her, and came to look after the orphaned Nora many years ago. Has had two letters from her own daughter. Does not complain, but loves Nora. Takes care of the children, and Nora clearly trusts her to go on doing so when she has gone.

12. There are a number of doors on the set. Write notes on each one that is mentioned and say where it leads, and how it is used in the play.

- Door to the hall: this is how everyone enters the flat. There is a door beyond to the outside, which we do not see, but we hear it slam in the final moments of the play. Nora enters at the beginning and leaves at the end through this door, but seems to be trapped for most of the action.
- Door to Helmer's study: Nora never goes in. Others can reach it via the hall, and come out of this door to greet Nora. The effect is to suggest it is forbidden to her.
- Door to the bedroom: not used until Nora goes to change her clothes in the last act. Her entrance in everyday clothes is all the more shocking for that.

13. How does Nora raise the money to pay off the loan? What difficulties does she encounter in doing so? Write brief notes in chronological order.

- She does embroidery and fancy-work. (Helmer does not like to see anything but dainty embroidery – has she had problems hiding more basic repair jobs?)
- She works as a copyist, which has to be done in secret. The previous winter, she had to pretend to be making Christmas decorations.
- She economises on her own clothes and on luxuries like Christmas presents; this is difficult as Helmer has expensive tastes and she dresses the children well.

14. How many times does Nora change her clothes, and why?

- She puts on a coloured shawl, part of the Capri outfit, to dance for Helmer and Rank. This is partly because it is only a rehearsal – but perhaps she prefers to choose her own style of dress.
- She wears the Capri dress to the party, with a 'large black shawl'. The dress is Helmer's choice. She is perhaps asserting her own taste and feelings with the black shawl.
- She puts on her 'everyday dress' to leave, plus outdoor clothes as the scene progresses. This is a practical choice – both for her new life, but also for the sober conversation she wants to have.

15. What subjects does Nora discuss with Dr Rank without Helmer's knowledge? Write a brief note on each saying why she does not talk to Helmer about each one.

- She tells him about her relationships with her father's servants. Helmer does not like her to talk about friends at all.
- She talks about his illness and its causes. This is not conventional behaviour and would shock Helmer.
- She speaks with him about his death. They agree Helmer cannot cope with the subject.

16. What do we know about the relationship between Krogstad and Mrs Linde? Make brief notes.

- They were once in love.
- She left him for a wealthier man to support her mother and small brothers.
- She thought it kindest to let Krogstad think she no longer cared.
- Both of them still care for the other.

17. Examine the time frame of the play, showing the main events and the time of day they take place.

- Act One:
  Christmas Eve: Nora gets home.
  Morning: Secures job for Mrs Linde; first visit from Krogstad.

- Act Two:
  Christmas Day afternoon: Mending the Capri dress
  Late afternoon: Nora and Dr Rank – the lamp is lit; second visit from Krogstad – he leaves the letter.
  About 5pm: Nora dances to distract Helmer from the mail; Mrs Linde cannot find Krogstad at home.
  Christmas dinner: 'Thirty-one hours to live'

- Act Three:
  Boxing Day nearly midnight: Mrs Linde and Krogstad talk; they decide to leave the letter.
  After midnight: Nora and Helmer return; he reads the letter; Krogstad returns the paper with the forged signature.
  Small hours of 27 December: Nora leaves.

18. Nora feels the men in her life have failed her. List her main reasons in the case of Helmer, Rank and her late father.

- HELMER: Took over her father's habit of treating her as a doll. Never allowed her to grow up. Does not stand up to Krogstad and say that he will take the blame – the 'miracle' Nora expected.
- RANK: Declares his love and alters the relationship. Unwittingly stops her asking him for money.
- FATHER: Treated her as a doll. Told her his opinions but did not encourage her to have her own. Let her go to Helmer as a kind of reward for helping him evade the law.

19. What happens to the Christmas tree? Write short notes on its appearance in each act, explaining what this adds to the play.

- Act One: A sign of optimism about their future prosperity as Nora enters, full of pleasure at Helmer's new job. Later in the act, a symbol of Nora's 'play-acting' to get what she wants from Helmer as she decorates it while trying to influence him about Krogstad's job.
- Act Two: Candles burnt out, presents stripped – how Nora feels she will be when she is older and no longer appeals to Helmer.
- Act Three: Tree may or may not be on stage, but will look as dishevelled as before as the marriage slowly unravels.

20. How do the other characters in the play describe Nora? Write down two or three quotations for each character.

- HELMER: 'squanderbird' (Act One, p. 24); 'a hypocrite, a liar – worse, worse – a criminal!' (Act Three, p. 93); 'my poor little Nora' (Act Three, p. 95)
- MRS LINDE: 'a child' (Act One, p. 33); 'you don't know what you're saying!' (Act Three, p. 74)
- RANK: 'a riddle to me' (Act Two, p. 69); 'the Spirit of Happiness' (Act Three, p. 90)
- KROGSTAD: 'dishonest' (Act One, p. 49); 'pampered little pretty' (Act Two, p. 73)
- NURSE: 'never had any mother but me' (Act Two, p. 56); 'beautiful' (Act Two, p. 56)

Section Two: Working towards the exam

1. Explore the function of clothing in the play.

- Denotes status: Helmer and Rank are superior to Krogstad; Mrs Linde is shabbier than Nora.
- Her outdoor clothes are visible but after her entrance she does not put them on till the end of the play, suggesting she is trapped.
- Her Capri dress shows Helmer's sexual desire and sense that she is his social inferior: 'my capricious little Capricienne' (Act Three, p. 85).
- Her change to 'everyday dress' (Act Three, p. 96) symbolises her seriousness about her new life, and the putting on of her outdoor clothes is a sign she is no longer trapped.

2. Helmer uses the word 'melodrama' about Nora. Which characters do you consider to behave melodramatically, and why?

- NORA is melodramatic in the literal sense. She makes use of music and dance to express her feelings. Her tarantella shows the fear she cannot speak about.
- She also speaks when alone, notably around the topic of suicide. 'Thirty-one hours to live' (Act Two, p. 79) describes her dilemma in very crude terms, but her intent is sincere.
- Her speech after Helmer goes to read his mail about 'the icy black water!' and the gesture of wrapping herself in his cloak (Act Three, p. 92) is in the tradition of a melodramatic sacrificial speech, but she does mean it. Her departure is more sober – but would shock its original audience more than the suicide speech.
- Nora's expectations are melodramatic. The 'miracle' she expects from Helmer is straight out of popular theatre.
- HELMER also plays out a gender stereotype from popular theatre. He sees himself as a noble hero protecting Nora with his 'broad wings' (Act Three, p. 96) – but only after he is in no danger from Krogstad, so the gesture is as empty as a cheap melodrama.
- His talk about 'honour' is also a fantasy that fits a melodrama.

3. 'The subplot is simply a device to prolong the suspense.' Do you agree?

- YES: If Krogstad is not going to take back his letter, there is no reason to motivate him for doing so.
- YES: Mrs Linde and Krogstad are functional characters.
- NO: It is important to show that an individual's actions affect many people, not just those close to them.
- NO: The idea that people can change is important for the main plot; we see it played out here and can draw conclusions about Nora and Helmer.

- NO: Both Krogstad and Mrs Linde are mirrors of Nora – what we learn about them helps us understand her.
- NO: Krogstad's change and Mrs Linde's insistence on honesty in Nora's marriage changes our view of the main plot.

4. Examine the role of money in the play.

- The plot hinges on the loan for which Nora has forged a signature.
- Money motivates behaviour: Krogstad and Mrs Linde have to survive and support families, Helmer is afraid of debt. Only Rank is disinterested, because he is dying.
- Money corrupts: Nora almost exploits Rank for his money, Helmer is so happy at being 'saved' that he fails to see what Nora is feeling, and Mrs Linde feels she has sold herself in the past.
- Money is at the root of the restrictions on women – Nora cannot legally borrow, has to hide her work as a married woman, has no automatic right to money from Helmer. She achieves partial independence only by leaving Helmer.
- Money perpetuates a class system: Mrs Linde, Krogstad and the nurse have all suffered because they are less well off than the Helmers.
- The forged signature and the money it represents is a symbol of the Helmers' marriage – secrets and lies about health, debt, work, all hidden.

5. 'The change we see in Nora in the final scene is too rapid to be believable.' Do you agree?

- YES: She is still childlike, expecting a 'miracle' until the end of the last act.
- YES: We never see her contemplate leaving Helmer, only melodramatic suicide.
- YES: Despite her lack of education, she argues her case so logically.
- NO: She has been working for some time and this has begun to change her.
- NO: She may well be tired of acting childishly to please Helmer – we know she thinks of this behaviour as 'tricks'.
- NO: Her last two encounters with Dr Rank are signs of moral growth.
- NO: She has been learning about the experience of Rank, Krogstad, Mrs Linde and the nurse in the course of the play and has profited.

Part Three: Characters and themes

Section One: Check your understanding

1. What does Helmer have to say about Nora's early life? What does she say about it?

- HE says that she was raised by an extravagent father and inherited his traits. SHE says that she wishes she had inherited 'more' of them (Act One, p. 27).
- HE says that he and her father loved her 'more than anything else in the world' (Act Three, p. 93). SHE agrees but talks about her liking for her father's servants and that 'there are some people whom one loves, and others whom it's almost more fun to be with' (Act Two, p. 69).
- HE is reticent about their courtship, but thinks he is now being 'punished' for helping Nora's father (and marrying Nora as a result). SHE thinks of herself as her father's doll, now Helmer's doll.

2. What was the former relationship between Mrs Linde and Krogstad? Can they restore it? Make brief notes.

- They were in love. She left him for a wealthier man to support her family.
- She heals the bitterness he feels about this by offering to work and care for him and his children – offering a chance to move on from the estrangement.
- She is convinced he can be a better man and is not troubled by his bad reputation.
- She suggests 'you and I need each other' (Act Three, p. 83) – a more solid basis for a partnership than the Helmers have.

3. Nora says that she needs to educate herself. Make a list of the skills or ideas she might need or want to learn.

- She needs to understand the law.
- She wants to look into religion because she no longer believes what she was taught.
- She wants genuine independence as a working woman, presumably building on the skills she has.
- 'I must try to satisfy myself which is right, society or I' (Act Three, p. 101) – she needs to discover what she thinks about politics. She now sees that there is such a thing as 'society' – in the debate in Act One she did not.
- She feels she is not qualified to educate her children – but perhaps she envisages that one day she may be.

4. What does Helmer expect of a wife? How does this affect his behaviour as a husband?

- To accept his ideas – so he cannot imagine duties as 'a human being' (Act Three, p. 100).
- To let him control money – so he treats the housekeeping as a gift to be asked for.
- To be attractive – so she must fit in with his sexual desires and be shown off.
- To find him enough – so she should not speak of old friends.

5. What economies does Nora make? Make a list and note whether they are successful.

- Dressing cheaply – yes, Helmer does not notice.
- Presents – yes, she buys cheap things, but feels bad about the nurse's gift.
- Housekeeping – no, Helmer 'likes to live well' (Act One, p. 36).

6. Which characters come into contact with the paper containing the signature? Make a list, with short notes on how each character might feel about it.

- NORA: signs name to protect her sick father, unaware that it is a crime. Takes a long time to grasp this point and thinks the law unreasonable.
- KROGSTAD: aware it is forged and uses this to blackmail Nora. Thinks her spoiled and silly, but also like himself, as he has done something similar.
- HELMER: finds out about it from Krogstad and considers Nora a criminal. When he receives it, he burns 'this filthy thing', delighted that *he* is 'saved' (Act Three, p. 95).
- THE MAID: has to get up to answer the door. Does not know what it is but cannot be very pleased at having her sleep spoiled (nobody apologises for this).

7. Find three instances in which a character behaves melodramatically – like a figure in a play. Make notes on the effect this has on them and on the characters observing them.

- Act Three, p. 81: Mrs Linde says that she will not give up her job at the bank, which was originally Krogstad's, because it would be no help. He says 'I'd do it all the same', which sounds like a very heroic gesture, although there is no possibility that he could ever make good on the promise. She treats this sceptically, and says that she has learned to be more practical. The debate is thrust into the realm of practical action, and they find a way forward by abandoning such dramatic talk.
- Act Three, p. 85: Helmer's narrative of the offstage tarantella. Here he shows himself to Mrs Linde as a powerful master of ceremonies presenting his wife as a spectacle. This makes him sexually assertive – he cannot wait to get rid of Mrs Linde, and later Rank, to be alone with Nora. Mrs Linde makes no comment – as an employee she cannot – but is probably aware that he is drunk. Nora is cowed and exhausted by the whole process.
- Act Three, p. 93: Nora throws a shawl over her head and prepares to take her own life. Helmer interrupts to tell her not to be 'theatrical' (Act Three, p. 93) Nora is not

pretending – this is the only way out she can think of. This suggests the limits of the marriage on both sides: she cannot tell him what she has done; he cannot deal with it rationally. His accusation is grounded in the fact that even her suicide would not help him, so it is a purely selfish response. 'Theatrical' to him evidently means 'making yourself the centre of attention, not me.'

8. What lies are told in the play, and why?
- Nora lies to Helmer about the macaroons – she sees no point in obeying Helmer when he cannot find out the truth.
- She tells Rank Mrs Linde bought them – he can eat them without guilt too.
- She told Helmer the money for his trip came from her father – she thinks it will harm his ego to know that she borrowed it.
- She pretends to waste money – she is paying off her debt to Krogstad.
- She lies about Krogstad visiting – she wants Helmer to think her intercession is spontaneous.
- Helmer pretends that he is dismissing Krogstad on ethical grounds – in fact he feels undermined by his over-familiarity.

9. Which character in the play do you think most closely resembles Nora in terms of their situation? Make brief notes explaining your reasons.
- KROGSTAD: has been a forger; cares about his children; increasingly feels he has nothing to lose and becomes more desperate.
- MRS LINDE: a working woman; has no family, but Nora feels she is about to lose hers.
- NURSE: a woman without power in a world controlled by men; lost her child, as Nora may lose hers.

10. Helmer thinks that morality is inherited. Is there any justification for his view in the play? Make a list of points for and against the idea.
- FOR: Mrs Linde speaks of Nora's 'spendthrift' ways at school – her father was extravagant and she is greedy for sweets.
- AGAINST: Helmer talks about this at much greater length, but is unaware of Nora's economies – if she was a spendthrift, she has grown out of it.
- FOR: Helmer speaks of Nora's father's 'recklessness and instability' and she certainly is reckless in forging the signature and is emotionally fragile throughout.
- AGAINST: These can be explained by immaturity – Nora grows up in the course of the play –she shows a growing sense of responsibility, towards Rank for example, and wants to save Helmer from the consequences of her actions.
- AGAINST: Rank has inherited his father's disease, but does not behave like him.

Section Two: Working towards the exam

1. 'Nora is a selfish character throughout the whole play.' Do you agree?
- YES: she talks about herself a great deal to Mrs Linde. When Mrs Linde tells her own story, Nora uses an account of her problems to compete.
- YES: she talks about 'strangers' (Act One, p. 25) and finds 'society' a bore (Act One, p. 40).
- YES: when Rank talks about his illness she is relieved to find that he does not know her situation, rather than thinking of him – 'Oh, it's you – ?' (Act Two, p. 64).
- YES: she does not consider the feelings of Helmer or the children when she leaves.
- NO: she learns to think about Krogstad's feelings, and shows genuine compassion for Dr Rank as she offers him a 'light' (Act Three, p. 90).
- NO: Helmer's remarks about 'constitutional liars' (Act One, p. 53) have made her feel she is a risk to her children and has gradually withdrawn from them. Her sense that she is 'not fitted to educate them' may be wrong, but it is genuine (ActThree, p. 99).
- NO: she cannot continue living with Helmer on the old terms. They both need to 'change so much' (Act Three, p. 104), as she realises.

2. Discuss the images of 'sickness' in the play. Does the play offer any definition of 'health'?
- There is a debate about 'people who are morally sick' in Act One (p. 39); Rank seems to think they are incurable, but Mrs Linde thinks they can be healed.
- Helmer speaks of 'evil' as a contagion (Act One, p. 53); he thinks children are corrupted by bad parents. Nora worries enough to withdraw from her children, but does not seem to endorse this view in general.
- Rank resents hereditary illness – not just his own, but the injustice of people suffering for 'someone else's sin' (Act Two, p. 65). He seems to see Nora as a force for healing and 'light'.
- Helmer has a fear of ugliness; he suggests his ideas about illness are not well founded. He seems fit himself – which he owes to Nora.
- Nora is physically healthy and athletic. She comes to realise that she can make choices and not be defined by a 'morally sick' father – is there a link?

3. Consider the ways in which Ibsen uses disguise, theatricality and role-play in *A Doll's House*.
- Nora is always 'dressed up' to some extent – even her ordinary dress hides its origins as the 'cheapest and plainest' (Act One, p. 37) as part of her secret economy. She constantly plays up to the 'skylark' image (Act One, p. 24) – but her anxiety makes this difficult and perhaps she resents it. She is effectively 'disguised' as the wife Helmer wants.

- At the same time, she acts like a character in popular melodrama – soliloquies such as the one ending 'Thirty-one hours to live' (Act Two, p. 79) have two functions: they give her some relief, and they also show the limits of her imagination. Not until the end can she discuss her situation rationally.

- Helmer performs the stereotype of masculinity – like his heroic 'broad wings' (Act Three, p. 96) – but cannot sustain it. He also uses Nora's tarantella to make her a spectacle, showing off his valuable possession.

- Krogstad's role is stereotyped but he constantly subverts it, e.g. by asking for a job in a bank rather than for riches or Nora's virtue.

- Four of the characters have a scene in which they sit and discuss their situation at a table – the least 'theatrical' moments in the play, but also the points of decision.

Part Four: Genre, Structure and Language

Section One: Check your understanding

1. Ibsen gives a number of stage directions to indicate that characters are doing something while they speak. List three of these and say what the action adds to our understanding.

- Act One: Nora hides the macaroons (p. 41) while silencing her guests. Rank is encouraging her to swear as Helmer approaches. It offers a visual, as well as verbal, demonstration of the way Nora habitually suppresses aspects of herself when Helmer is there – and a comic confirmation that the guests collaborate in deceiving him.

- Act Two (p. 56): Nora unpacks her Capri outfit while saying she dare not go out. This gives the actress a chance to move energetically, shaking it out and flinging it aside, which reflects her emotional state, and also lodges the dress firmly as a symbol of Helmer's control.

- Act Three: Nora lights a cigar for Dr Rank (p. 90). It gives her a chance to move close to him; he will pick up her words and thank her for a 'light' that is spiritual as well as physical. It also shows Ibsen's concern to use light on the stage – the bright flame lights both Rank and Nora in a tight circle that is for them alone.

2. Find three examples of women's financial dependency on men in the play. Make brief notes on how it affects them.

- Act One (p. 26): Nora has to ask Helmer for money as a Christmas present. He dispenses what he sees fit, rather than what she needs – and she always has to charm it out of him.

- Act One: Mrs Linde needs Nora's influence to secure a job at the bank, although Helmer must think it is his idea. It would be more difficult for a woman to get work through more formal channels.

- Act Two: the nurse says 'That good-for-nothing didn't lift a finger' (p. 56) to help her when she became pregnant. She had to give up her own child as the only work available was that of wet nurse to the orphaned Nora. Her life was totally changed.

3. Find a conversation or speech which acts as exposition for the audience. Do you find it convincing as natural dialogue? Make brief notes.

- In the conversation which begins 'Oh Torvald, surely we can let ourselves go a little bit this year!' (Act One, p. 24) the focus appears to be on Nora's extravagance, or at least Helmer's view of it. His sudden appearance sets this moment up as comic. The information provided – about his new job, his salary, and when it begins – is part of this good-humoured marital debate about money and comes quite naturally. When we know all this, we are aware that this is a modestly prosperous household that has had some financial insecurity.

4. Find three examples of a character communicating through subtext. Make brief notes to explain the feelings or ideas beneath the words.

- Nora's remark to Rank, 'You mean he was too fond of asparagus and *foie gras*?' (Act Two, p. 65) is effectively saying, 'I know your father had a sexually transmitted disease, but of course it would be very improper to speak of it. However, I am not ignorant of such subjects and I know you respect me for that.'

- Nora's tarantella (Act Two, p. 77) is apparently a chance for Helmer to play teacher, but her wild dance is actually showing her terror at what will happen when Helmer knows about the forged signature. Nobody interprets it correctly – Rank even wonders if she is pregnant.

- Helmer's demonstration of embroidery (Act Three, p. 86) is partly a way of venting his resentment of a visitor he finds a bore – he attacks her knitting instead of her. It is also an assertion of male superiority; he shows the woman that he *could* do all this much better than she could, if only he condescended to learn.

5. Find an episode in which Nora tries and fails to express what she thinks to another person. What do you think is the problem in this case? Make brief notes.

- In Act One Nora asks Helmer's advice about her dress for the party as a prelude to raising the subject of Krogstad. She says, 'It all seems so stupid and meaningless.' (p. 52) This is a very strong remark to make about a party dress – is she trying to say that Helmer's behaviour over Krogstad is stupid and meaningless? Or might she be referring to her habitual playacting and childishness? Helmer gives her no help here, but she seems to want an adult conversation.

6. Make short notes on Nora's first entrance in each act. What do we learn about her state of mind from each?

- Act One: Happy and excited about Christmas – perhaps about having almost paid off the debt to Krogstad. At this moment she could be the heroine of a comedy.

- Act Two: There as the curtain rises, apparently having failed to go out despite the presence of outdoor clothes. Afraid of what the next day will bring – a note from Krogstad to Helmer about the forged signature. On edge, and not calmed by the nurse or Mrs Linde when they enter.

- Act Three: A delayed entrance – we hear the party going on and are anticipating her arrival while Krogstad and Mrs Linde talk. Reluctant to enter – physically dragged in? Trouble will begin as soon as Helmer opens his mail. Capri dress contrasts with her evident unhappiness. Helmer is concerned to 'present' her to Mrs Linde and show off her beauty and Nora may look troubled at this. The happier he is, the greater his shock will be.

7. List the appearances made by the maid and make short notes on each to say what they add to our understanding of the Helmer household.

- ACT ONE: She helps Nora with the Christmas tree. We learn that her name is Helen – Nora is on good terms with her. (p. 23)

- Announces a 'stranger' – Mrs Linde – and lets Rank straight through to see Helmer. (p. 28) The first sign of Helmer's reluctance to engage with new people.

- Krogstad insists on seeing Helmer (p. 38), leaving the maid at a loss – the first sign Nora has a secret. Later he will ignore Helen completely and come in unannounced.

- Helps with the Christmas tree, which Nora intends to decorate while trying to influence Helmer not to dismiss Krogstad. Puzzled, maybe – this is earlier than Nora planned to set up the tree – she/we may recall the different spirit in which Nora first came in. (p. 51)

- ACT TWO: In this act friends come and go without being announced; is she on light duties for Christmas? Sent with a letter dismissing Krogstad as Helmer indulges in a moment of spite. Does her face reflect surprise at being sent running errands on Christmas Day? Or is Helmer often given to peremptory commands like this?

- Brings in the lamp for Nora and Rank just after Rank has declared his love. (p. 68) Nora shows that she is in command of the situation – but the maid may show awareness that something is going on, adding to the charged atmosphere.

- Admits Krogstad – this is done in whispers, using the back door. The sense of menace is heightened by the fact Nora is not troubling to hide Krogstad from Helmer – surely the maid cannot believe he is a Christmas 'surprise' as Nora claims? (p. 70)

- ACT THREE: Answers the door in the small hours to receive Krogstad's letter returning the forged document. She is 'half dressed' (p. 94) – and must be aware that something strange is going on. Helmer snatches the letter she has announced as being for Nora. May well look shocked – it is a real sign of the disintegration of the household when husband and wife show no solidarity.

8. Make a list of the costumes worn by the men and write brief notes to say how they show their status and their character.

- HELMER: We are not told what he wears at home, but he does not change when going out to the bank; we should assume he is wearing a formal dark suit. Suggests he spends much of his time at home working and perhaps does not draw much distinction between work and home. Nora says that he likes 'to live well' (Act One, p. 36) – his clothes are not likely to be cheap. They will stress his new status as bank manager.

- At the party, he wears an evening suit with a black coat over it (Act Three, p. 84). Suggests he thinks himself above 'dressing up' – he leaves that to Nora; this makes him conspicuous at a fancy-dress party, reflecting his egotistic nature.

- RANK: He wears a fur coat (Act One, p. 42), which he warms before putting it on. Shows he is quite wealthy – richer than Helmer – but also that he is physically frail and suffers in cold weather.

- KROGSTAD: His 'overcoat, heavy boots and a fur cap' (Act Two, p. 70) make him look large and menacing – perhaps he knows this. They are thick and bulky to deal with the extreme cold. A contrast to the finer tailoring of the other men – they have more stylish ways of keeping warm and perhaps do not have to travel so far. Krogstad's clothes will be cheap but functional.

9. Ibsen makes use of a lighted lamp at several points. Make brief notes explaining what this brings to the stage picture.

- Act Two, p. 68: Marks the time of day as late afternoon. Calling for the lamp helps Nora break up the intense conversation with Rank, and brings moral 'light' into a situation she thinks is getting out of hand. Creates a circle of light in which the two of them sit and talk quietly. The audience will focus on it closely – this is the most intimate conversation of the play so far.

- Act Three, p. 80: Mrs Linde sits at the table with the lamp lit. Here she will have her conversation with Krogstad – and Nora and Helmer will have their last talk. Suggests it is very late, with the rest of the stage quite dim. Focuses our attention on these quiet duologues. New placing of the furniture suggests that Mrs Linde has arranged it – she has set the stage for a final reckoning between both couples, like a stage manager placing a spotlight.

10. Choose three comic moments and write brief notes on their dramatic effect.

- Act One: Nora, Mrs Linde and Rank eat macaroons (p. 40), giving a comic coda to the debate about morality – they know that Helmer would not like this. Some of the laughter comes from Nora's deftness in lying – she says they are from Mrs Linde – and some from the way the others are abruptly brought down from the moral high ground. A chance for the actors to show physical comedy as they hastily gobble them down on Helmer's entrance.

- Act Two: Helmer sends Krogstad a letter of dismissal. Although this is a tense moment for Nora, the slow uncovering of Helmer's real motives for the letter – snobbery, insecurity and a desire not to look as if he obeys his wife – are comic. The more desperately he tries to assert himself, the more ridiculous he looks, culminating in the childish 'There now, little Miss Obstinate' (p. 63). The comedy stops any suggestion of melodrama; we will hear about the real implications of Helmer's act from Krogstad himself.

- Act Three: Helmer's tipsy presentation of knitting and embroidery. A bold choice by Ibsen – we anticipate a painful final confrontation later, but cannot help laughing. It stresses the problems of this marriage – not just Helmer's pomposity and possessiveness, but the way he is completely oblivious to the feelings of others. Nora is in agony, and he does not notice. The suspense is heightened. We may feel some affection for the buffoonish Helmer, which modifies our shock at his selfish behaviour later.

···

Section Two: Working towards the exam
···

1. The play tells the story of one family's Christmas. Explore the relationship between the festivities and the action of the play.

- At first sight, the play looks like a happy domestic comedy involving a wife's extravagance – not too serious, as the husband is doing well. The play uncovers the emotional struggles beneath this surface and the breakup is more poignant for the festive setting.

- Some characters are drawn into the family circle – Rank, and to some extent Mrs Linde. This underlines the 'outsider' status of Krogstad, a dark thread running through the story. His every appearance is frightening to Nora – and he also seems to obsess Helmer, who dismisses him on Christmas Day.

- It is a time for celebration. For Nora, this aids her pretences – she uses decorating the tree, rehearsing her dance, serving champagne, to distract Helmer, as well as make the day festive.

- Christmas often involves disguise and masquerade. Nora's Capri dress is associated with her identity and she has a complex relationship with it.

- Her last conversation with Rank is about what they will wear next year – he indicates that they will both be their true selves – he dead, she the 'Spirit of Happiness'.

- Christmas marks the darkest point of the year and the return of the sun after the solstice. The play progresses from morning to darkness, with the promise of dawn as Nora leaves.

- Nora is a 'lightbringer' to Dr Rank, with the lamp and the lit cigar. Despite the tragic aspects of the marriage breakup, the play ends on optimism and possibility.

2. Choose three entrances or exits you think are particularly interesting and explain what they contribute to the play.

- One of the most important entrances is that of the **children in Act One**. Nora is at her most freespirited. A great deal of bustle – the guests and Helmer are leaving as the children arrive. Whatever the stresses on her, Nora can still be happy.

- It is a cue for an eruption of activity, the most vigorous in the play until the tarantella. Nora chases the children all round the apartment – into rooms we do not see used again, until she changes her clothes. She seems in control of the world around her.

- **Krogstad's entrance** changes this. It comes as a shock– visitors so far have been announced. It is a shock to Nora – we have some knowledge of why she dislikes Krogstad. But it is also a comic moment, with Nora interrupted in the midst of a childish game.

- The contrast between these two entrances shows Ibsen's skill in constantly changing the mood while never ceasing to develop suspense. The space is first dominated by Nora, in command of her little family, and then by Krogstad, who seizes the right to come and go as he likes.

- **Nora's last entrance** in the play is one we look forward to – the prelude to her confrontation with Helmer. Ibsen delays it through the conversation between Mrs Linde and Krogstad. Her reluctance to enter contrasts with her first happy entrance in Act One.

- Her costume is important – she is wearing the Capri dress for the first time. It contrasts with her unhappiness and stresses that Nora is a prisoner – the party is upstairs, and she is only wearing a shawl, not a coat. She has still failed to get out of the trap.

- Helmer's irrepressible good spirits as he drags her in are both funny and chilling. He is absurd in his drunken pomposity, but also unaware of Nora's feelings, or those of Mrs Linde, who knows what is coming.

3. Find three instances where Nora is unable to say what she wants, and suggest the reasons for this.

- The play might be described as Nora's journey into articulacy. Her first word is 'hide', and she spends a great deal of time keeping secrets. She also panders to Helmer's desire for a child-wife, with mutual games in which she enacts animals. She intends never to tell him about raising the money for Italy – unless he grows bored with her.

- We know she finds this frustrating, e.g. when she admits to a desire to swear in front of him. This is comic, but also an important insight into the relationship. It is not that she wants to use swear words – she is uninhibited with Rank and Mrs Linde – but that she wants to shock Helmer; she wants to change things between them. Is there some unspoken resentment about hiding the practical, competent side of herself she has expressed to Mrs Linde? Is her appetite for sweets a sign of suppressed rage?

- A second instance of frustration arises when she tries to raise the subject of Krogstad. Helmer sees him leave so knows she is lying about seeing nobody. She thus has to approach the topic with care – perhaps we see her irritation. It emerges when she says fancy dress is 'stupid and meaningless' (Act One, p. 52) – perhaps trying to communicate what she really feels? Or criticise Helmer's behaviour? Or raise some of the subjects covered in the debate between her guests earlier? Helmer crushes her with a patronising remark about 'little Nora' (Act One, p. 54).

- She has to be careful asking for information and has to endure Helmer's sermon about lying – he might not be so vehement if he knew what was at stake. Terrified, she decides to keep her own secret. She will pass judgement on herself by refusing to see the children.

- Nora cannot ask Dr Rank to lend her the money, because he has declared his love for her. This is a different kind of silencing – it stems from a moral insight on her part, not from the need to keep her secret. The first time that Nora has made an ethical decision – the problems of others up to now have been boring. She decides to keep her friend, rather than exploit him. It will mean that they can later say a loving goodbye.

- As a moment of growth, it is also a milestone in her journey to become the articulate Nora of Act Three. Here she speaks of the rights and wrongs of her upbringing in a clear and rational way – this would be beyond the frustrated wife who wants to swear in Act One.

Part Five: Contexts and Interpretations

Section One: Check your understanding

1. Choose a section from a work from a different period which explores the nature of marriage. Compare it with *A Doll's House* and list the differences you notice.

- Chaucer's *The Merchant's Tale* assumes that the only real problem in marriage is that of fidelity. *A Doll's House* takes a more complex view.

- *The Merchant's Tale* is told from one, highly biased, point of view. Although Nora is the central character, we know a great deal about the other characters – their interactions are important, part of the fabric of the Helmers' marriage.

- We are free to form our own view of Nora's decision to leave – audiences have always disagreed. *The Merchant's Tale* expects cynical conclusions about marriage – this will only be questioned outside the tale itself.

- In *A Doll's House* Ibsen consciously puts his own society on stage – this is a marriage with problems and advantages typical of a middle-class home in Norway in the 1870s. *The Merchant's Tale* is set in a stylised world of classical gods, suggesting the teller thinks he is uttering universal truths about marriage.

2. What do we know about Helmer's economic status in his world? Write a short report.

- Helmer has practised as a lawyer and has now been made vice-president of the local bank – a significant step up the economic and social ladder, although his new salary does not begin for another four months. He owns a modest apartment and keeps his wife and three children, as well as paying two live-in servants. He has significant power over the lives of others: he can grant loans, and has power to hire or dismiss people at will. He exercises this over Mrs Linde and Krogstad. He is evidently solvent and holds great store by remaining so.

- This has meant that his wife has incurred a debt of £250 – a large sum – on his behalf, for which he will be legally liable if she should default on it. Thus, although he is a good credit risk in terms of ability and income, his morbid sensibilities about debt are exaggerated and cause problems; a more balanced approach would be better.

3. What challenges would the play offer a nineteenth-century actress? Make a short list.

- The role of Nora requires the ability to shift between emotional intensity and light comedy – at a time when actresses in stock companies tended to be thought of as *ingénues* or as comediennes.

- It also demands a grasp of the acting style of popular theatre, with strong emotion expressed in heightened language and vigorous gestures. However, in the play these reflect the tendency of Nora to self-dramatise.

- They contrast with the overall performance style of restrained naturalism. Ibsen is a pioneer in this respect; the actress will also be innovative.

- An actress playing Nora would need to cope with being a controversial figure for the audience and their mixed responses to her – from extreme hostility to strong identification with her problems.

4. Who would you describe as the most powerful character in the play? List your reasons.

- HELMER: has the economic power; can hire or dismiss people; can make decisions about what happens to the children; has a hold over his father-in-law that has enabled him to marry Nora.

- He is also part of an emerging new class in Norway, the petite bourgeoisie. Though the country is under the control of the judiciary and the armed forces, this is a significant social group with votes and influence. The only person who might rival him is Rank, but as a dying man he is not in a position to exercise much power.

5. How is the Norwegian setting important to the action? List your ideas.

- The Norwegian winter, especially around the solstice, has a long night and a short day. This parallels Nora's transition from trouble into self-realisation.
- The emphasis on typically Norwegian Christmas festivities helps to shape the plot: Christmas Eve, the day of present-giving, stresses the importance of the children. Christmas Day draws together friends, and allows Nora serious conversations with Rank and Mrs Linde. Boxing Day opens up to a wider social circle, with the party.
- The image of the cold, dark fjord and the bodies in the spring thaw (Act Two, p. 73) is specific to Norway; it makes Nora's terror and ambivalence towards suicide very real.
- The rapid industrialisation of the country has created people like Mrs Linde. She is a possible role model for Nora, but would not have existed in Norway twenty years before.

6. How might an adaptation of the play tell you something about the period that produced it?

- The play has the status of a 'classic' – it will be performed in a variety of cultural settings and is likely to be subject to interpretation.
- Nora's struggle takes place in a setting of relative affluence. It may therefore speak to a society where women have limited rights but which is not without the means to change it. For example, the 1935 production in China by Jiang Qing was seen as the beginning of cultural modernity – part of a resistance to traditional practices such as foot-binding.
- There is a profound concern with freedom of speech in the play. This made Nora a key figure in Chile during the Pinochet regime. Period clothes and setting here underlined the 'classic' status, so were not overtly subversive, but Nora's final eloquence suggested that the people could find a voice.
- More radical adaptations, e.g. the Kurdish translation which parallels the story with a Kurdish folk-tale, or the 2012 Chilean *In Pursuit of Nora Helmer*, suggest that a more direct confrontation with cultural developments and conventions is needed to let the play speak to a different society.

7. Compare two different critical views and say which you agree with most. List your reasons.

- Some critics claim *A Doll's House* is 'nothing to do with the sexes'. (Michael Meyer, *Henrik Ibsen, The Farewell to Poetry*, Granada, 1971, p. 266) The main point of this argument is that the characters are 'universal' in their appeal.
- Feminists like Joan Templeton would say that the power of the play 'lies not beyond but in its feminism' (*Ibsen's Women*, CUP, 2001, p. 123).
- Although it would be possible to have a play about a man freeing himself from a domineering wife, its effect would be quite different.

- Nora is a product of specific pressures. The position of women was changing, so that a new freedom was possible, but would require great courage for a woman to attain it. It is essential that Nora is a female character – a man would be legally able to incur a debt and he would get custody of his children if his marriage ended.
- Many early critics who resisted the play offered alternative versions – they could envisage the possibility of a Helmer delighted at losing his wife or a Nora who could not manage independence – but not a different balance of the sexes.
- The play is about Nora's own relationship with her gender – how she feels 'like a man' when working, for instance, and what she feels about motherhood.

8. List the women in the play in order of social power, with reasons.

- NORA: As the wife of the vice-president of the bank she has some influence, though she has to make Helmer think her ideas are his own; she has the potential to make money and be independent; she has some access to Helmer's money; she is able to charm people like Dr Rank and make friends of all classes; she has to give up security and children, but is confident in the future.
- MRS LINDE: She has earned her own living with some success; she is still recovering from a bad marriage which involved bankruptcy; she has the strength to make the first move in relationships to get what she wants.
- NURSE, ANNE-MARIE: She was betrayed by her first lover and had to give up her child; she depends on Helmer for her livelihood, though Nora makes it clear she is the best person to care for the children.

9. Look at a review of the play from the nineteenth century. What does the reviewer take for granted about the relationships between men and women? Make a brief list.

- Assumes Nora, a charming and comic character in the first acts, cannot become the woman of the last act. This suggests that characters cannot radically change.
- Assumes that the unequal relations between men and women, on which the plot depends, are 'natural' rather than problematic.
- Assumes that 'marriage' is capable of a single definition, rather than being an institution which might change.
- Assumes the break-up of a marriage is a disaster, rather than a sad but sometimes necessary process.

10. At what points in the play do you think Nora and Helmer conform most closely to the gender roles their society endorses? Make a brief list.

- In her first scene with Helmer, Nora is childish and manipulative – 'feminine' qualities in much nineteeth-century literature.

- Her tarantella shows her enacting the stereotype of woman as a creature driven by emotion rather than reason. Rank thinks she may be pregnant and Helmer that she is 'like a child' (p. 78).
- Helmer plays the role of breadwinner with enthusiasm in Act One, assuming that his earnings are for him to give or withhold, rather than being the household budget.
- In the last act he strikes the pose of a 'man of honour', refusing to break a code women cannot understand. Nora's brisk deflation, 'Millions of women have done it' (p. 102), makes no sense to him.

Section Two: Working towards the exam

1. 'A Doll's House is the first truly modern play about marriage.' Do you find it 'modern'? Give your reasons for or against.

- AGAINST: The plot is now dated. Nora could incur a debt without her husband's knowledge. She could leave him and keep the children. This means that it is difficult to recapture the original excitement at how radical her action is.
- The play is so rooted in nineteenth-century Norway – clothes, set, ideas – that it can only be enjoyed as a period piece.
- FOR: Arguably, the play marks a real change in the way people thought about the position of women.
- It constantly undercuts the theatricality of many scenes, e.g. Nora is criticised by Helmer for being 'melodramatic' (Act Three, p. 94) but he then makes a very theatrical speech saying, 'Your wildly beating little heart shall find peace with me' (Act Three, p. 96) only moments after announcing that their marriage will continue in name only. This kind of metatheatre is more common in our time than Ibsen's.
- The play radically redefines marriage by looking forward to a 'miracle of miracles' (Act Three, p. 104) that would make it a true partnership.
- It is constantly revived and adapted at times and places where the nature of marriage, the role of women or the question of free speech is being questioned.

2. 'All the relationships in the play are based in some way upon economic power.' Do you agree? Give reasons for or against.

- AGAINST: The relationship between Nora and Helmer is highly individual. Their 'skylark and squirrel' games are not about economics but about their personalities.
- The play could be seen as being about a woman who refuses to grow up until circumstances force her to – the debt is just a mechanism.
- Helmer's neurosis about debt: 'Suppose … a tile fell off a roof on to my head –' (Act One, p. 24), is pathological. It is this that drives his treatment of Nora, not a lack of actual purchasing power.

- FOR: It is no coincidence that Helmer works in a bank – an organisation which shapes people's lives by lending money or giving interest. The plot hinges on a debt (£250) and what that means to different characters affects how they treat one another.
- Nora's intimate relationships have been shaped by her father's financial dishonesty and Helmer's fear of debt. Her secrecy and fear stem from hiding the debt from them.
- We are constantly made aware what money can buy – Nora's cheap but stylish dress, Christmas gifts, the Italian holiday – and how it makes relationships easier. It is always contrasted with the struggles of those with nothing – Mrs Linde's first marriage to help her family, her poverty as a widow, Krogstad's desperation to support his children, even through blackmail.

3. 'Helmer is nothing but a collection of stereotypes of masculinity.' Do you agree? List your reasons for or against and suggest how this might affect the actor's performance.

- FOR: Helmer displays many instances of stereotypical masculinity: concern for his honour (Act Three, p. 102); sexual possessiveness and pride, when he shows off Nora's tarantella; reluctance to discuss his work with his wife in a critical spirit.
- He sees parenthood as a mother's job, evading interaction with the children in Act One. At the same time he sees his power to withhold them from Nora as his right.
- He displays sexual desire, but not much emotion around the end of his marriage.
- It took courage for early actors to play him unsympathetically – the audience would not automatically side with Nora; to treat Helmer as a victim would unbalance the play.
- AGAINST: The actor needs to show us the vulnerability of the man who has already collapsed from overwork and is haunted by the idea of debt.
- Helmer's pomposity – 'There now, little Miss Obstinate' (Act Two, p. 63) – is comic. If the actor is young, it will make him seem childlike, even endearing at times.
- He is not emotionless; rather, he lacks the ability to articulate emotion. When he loses Nora and appeals to outside forces like the Law and the Church, this is the only language he knows.
- This lack of imagination is arguably his tragedy. He has never thought through those stereotypes any more than Nora has thought through the feminine ones that shape her actions.
- Some noted recent Helmers have played the final scene as a broken man, e.g. Owen Teale and Trevor Eve.

MARK SCHEME

Use this page to assess your answer to the **Practice task** on page 102.

Look at the elements listed for each Assessment Objective. Examiners will be looking to award the highest grades to the students who meet the majority of these criteria. If you can meet two to three elements from each AO, you are working at a good level, with some room for improvement to a higher level.*

> **Compare the ways in which the writers of your two chosen texts [here, *A Doll's House* compared with *The Kite Runner*] present rebellion against those in power. You must relate your discussion to relevant contextual factors.**

A01	Articulate informed, personal and creative responses to literary texts, using associated concepts and terminology, and coherent, accurate written expression.	• You make a range of clear, relevant points about rebellion against those in power. • You use a range of literary terms correctly, e.g. irony, imagery, **metatheatre**, dialogue. • You address the topic clearly across both texts, outlining your thesis and providing a clear conclusion. • You signpost and link fluently your ideas about rebellion both within and across the two texts. • You offer a personal interpretation which is insightful, well-argued and convincing.
A02	Analyse ways in which meanings are shaped in literary texts.	• You explain the techniques and methods Ibsen uses to present women's rebellion against those in power, through potential role models or mirrors for Nora and visual images, such as Nora's changes of clothing. • You explain in detail how such examples shape meaning in both texts, e.g. how both Amir's friend Hassan and his wife offer him role models; how the flying kites change from an image of competition to one of freedom and reconciliation. • You comment on genre, language, setting and structure in a thoughtful, sustained way.
A03	Demonstrate understanding of the significance and influence of the contexts in which literary texts are written and received.	• You demonstrate your understanding of the social construction of gender roles. • Literary context: how both works need to be read in the light of other texts – the **well-made plays** of the nineteenth century, the story of Sohrab and Rustum. • Historical or social contexts: the rise of feminism and the New Woman, the changes in Afghanistan after the coming of the Taliban.
A04	Explore connections across literary texts.	• You make relevant links between characters and ideas within a text, noting how, for example, both Nora and Hassan find new language in order to articulate their case against the prevailing opinion. • You make critical judgements about the approach to rebellion in both texts, drawing comparisons and contrasts, for example 'asserting oneself by writing stories, flying kites, or flirting in witty and allusive language'.
A05	Explore literary texts informed by different interpretations.	• Where appropriate, you incorporate and comment on critics' views of the extent to which the texts can be seen in particular ways, e.g. how Shaw remarked on the way the slam of the door in *A Doll's House* echoed round the world. • You assert your own independent view clearly.

* This mark scheme gives you a broad indication of attainment, but check the specific mark scheme for your paper/task to ensure you know what to focus on.